Medal in the British Museum.   Busts of Christ and St. Paul.

THE

MEDALLIC PORTRAITS

OF CHRIST

THE FALSE SHEKELS

THE THIRTY PIECES OF SILVER

By G. F. HILL

FELLOW OF THE BRITISH ACADEMY

OXFORD

AT THE CLARENDON PRESS

1920

Oxford University Press

London   Edinburgh   Glasgow   New York

Toronto   Melbourne   Cape Town   Bombay

Humphrey Milford *Publisher to the University*

PREFACE

OF the essays included in this volume, those which deal with the Medallic Portraits of Christ and False Shekels were originally published in the *Reliquary and Illustrated Archaeologist* in 1902, 1904, and 1905. Constant inquiries concerning these subjects are addressed to the British Museum and doubtless to other similar institutions. It seemed, therefore, worth while to place on record what is known about them ; not so much, it must be confessed, in the hope of dissipating certain picturesque superstitions, which continue to show every sign of a long and happy life ; but rather to make it easier for scholars to answer the inquiries addressed to them. At the same time, some few of those who are curious in such matters are interested to learn the truth ; others are occasionally convinced by the printed word where the mere assurance of a Museum official would be received with passionate incredulity. The research, once undertaken, proved to have attractions of its own, although the portion concerned with the medals of the later sixteenth century has been worked out more from a sense of duty than because of any interest in the banal types produced in that period ; and the whole is, I fear, anything but easy reading.

The essay on the Thirty Pieces of Silver, being more or less akin to the others, seemed not unfitting to accompany them. It was read before the Society of Antiquaries of London in 1904, and printed in *Archaeologia*, vol. lix.

I am indebted to Messrs. George Allen & Co., the present proprietors of the *Reliquary*, and to the Council of the Society of Antiquaries, for their kind permission to republish the essays, which have been revised and in great part rewritten in the light of more recent investigation. My thanks are also due to the Directors of foreign museums and to the private collectors, by whose courtesy I am able to publish illustrations of a number of pieces not represented in the British Museum ; and to my colleague Mr. O. M. Dalton, who has been so good as to read the proofs and make various useful suggestions.

G. F. HILL.

BRITISH MUSEUM,
March, 1920.

LECTORES DOCILES PAGINA NOSTRA VOCAT

Godfrey of Viterbo

LIST OF ILLUSTRATIONS

I

MEDALLIC PORTRAITS OF CHRIST

I. The Fifteenth Century

'Ω φιλτάτη πρόσοψις, ὦ ποθουμένη
ὡραιότης ἄρρητος ὑπὲρ πᾶν γένος,
εἰκὼν ἄγραφος ἀγράφου μορφώματος.—*Christus Patiens.*

THE question of the artistic development of the portrait of Christ, in itself sufficiently intricate, has been so much complicated by contributions from writers more remarkable for their piety than for their sense of evidence, that it is necessary to apologize for attacking it once more. My excuse must be that I propose practically to limit myself to the medallic portraits of the Renaissance, only incidentally dealing with earlier representations, and to ignore altogether, as a matter which can hardly be proved one way or the other, the question whether the numerous portraits bear any resemblance to the actual countenance of Christ. There is, I take it, no doubt that nearly all later representations have been much influenced by the various literary descriptions [1] of Christ, of which the earliest seems to be that given by John of Damascus, who died about 754.[2] Better known is the famous letter supposed to have been written by Publius Lentulus to the Roman Senate.[3] A third description is given

---

[1] Cf. F. X. Kraus, *Gesch. der christlichen Kunst*, i, p. 177.

[2] *Epist. ad Theophilum*, c. 3 (Migne, *Patrol., Ser. Gr.*, vol. 95, p. 350).

[3] See J. P. Gabler, *Kleinere theolog. Schriften* (Ulm, 1831), ii, pp. 628 f. Gabler comes to the conclusion that the letter was concocted by some monk of the thirteenth or fourteenth century. It appears for the first time in print, although not under the name of Lentulus,

in a tract headed, 'Ex gestis Anselmi colliguntur forma et mores beatae Mariae et eius unici filii Iesu', on the last page of an undated edition (end of fifteenth century) of St. Anselm's *Opuscula*; but it is not acknowledged among his genuine works. The current assumption, therefore, that it goes back to Anselm's time is unfounded. I have not been able to trace any manuscript containing it earlier than the fourteenth century.

by Nicephorus Callisti (Xanthopoullos), who died about 1350.[1]

John of Damascus describes Christ as having meeting eyebrows, fine eyes, long nose, curly hair, stooping shoulders, fresh complexion, black beard, and a skin the colour of wheat, as well as other characteristics which do not concern us here. Nicephorus agrees in most particulars with John, adding that his hair was

Fig. 1.—Medal by Matteo de' Pasti. Collection of Mr. Henry Oppenheimer.

golden, not very thick, inclining to curliness ; eyebrows black, not much curved ; beautiful eyes, bright and inclined to brown ; long nose ; beard golden, and not very long ; hair of the head long ; attitude somewhat stooping ; complexion wheat-coloured ; face not round but rather pointed below, and slightly rubicund. The letter of Lentulus describes his hair as nut-brown, smooth to the ears, curling on the shoulders, parted in the middle ; his forehead smooth and serene ; his face without wrinkle or blemish, slightly rubicund ; nose and teeth good ; full beard, like his hair, not long, but forked in the middle, &c., &c.

[1] *Hist. Eccl.* i. 40 (Migne, vol. 145, p. 748).

The head of Christ first makes its appearance on coins in the reign of Justinian II (A.D. 685–95).[1] He is represented with long flowing hair, moustache and beard, and a cross behind the head. It is a full-face representation, such as was only to be expected at the time, when it is quite the exception to find a profile portrait on a coin. The facing bearded bust of Christ, with various modifications, continues in use in Byzantium down

Fig. 2.—Sketch for Medal of Christ in the Recueil Vallardi.
From Heiss, Méd. de la Ren.

to the very end of the coinage in 1448. The beardless bust, also facing, does not appear until the reign of Manuel I (A.D. 1143–80).[2] These facing types had no influence whatever on the Renaissance attempts at portraying the Saviour, which, so far as medals are concerned, are invariably in profile, usually to the left. The busts of Christ on the coins, in fact, are merely examples, on a small scale, of the orthodox Byzantine iconography of Christ, which Italian art discarded as soon as it felt able to do so.

[1] W. Wroth, *Catalogue of the Imperial Byzantine Coins in the British Museum* (1908), ii, p. 331, nos. 11 ff.   [2] W. Wroth, *op. cit.*, ii, p. 566.

The medals with which I propose to deal may be divided roughly into two classes, corresponding to the fifteenth and sixteenth centuries.

The earliest of which we have any knowledge (fig. 1) is the work of the medallist Matteo de' Pasti of Verona, Pisanello's most distinguished pupil.[1] His various medals of Sigismondo Pandolfo Malatesta and Isotta Atti bear dates from 1446 to 1457, and it is improbable that the medal with the head of Christ is much later than 1460. Its description is as follows :

Fig. 3.—Repoussé Medallion in Victoria and Albert Museum.

Obv.— · IESVS · CHRISTVS · DEVS · DEI · FILIVS · HVMANI · GENERIS · SALVATOR · Bust of Christ l., with plain circular nimbus seen in perspective ; the hair is brushed back from the forehead and falls in curls on the shoulders ; beard full, but not forked or long ; moustache full ; whiskers slightly curly. He wears a vest and cloak.

Rev.— · OPVS · MATTHAEI · PASTII · VERONENSIS · The dead Christ, seen in half-figure in his tomb ; his head supported by a putto ; on the left, another putto, weeping, with hands uplifted ; behind, the cross.

Bronze, 93 mm.   Stops in the legends, inverted triangles.

The obverse of this medal bears considerable resemblance to a drawing in the Recueil Vallardi in the Louvre. The majority of the drawings in this album are from the hand of Pisanello himself ; but to any one acquainted with the work of that master, it is clear that this particular design, which I reproduce here (fig. 2) after Heiss (p. 28), is not from his hand. The treatment of the hair and beard differs from that on the medal ; the bust has

[1] See especially A. Heiss, *Les Médailleurs de la Renaissance : Léon-Baptiste Alberti, Matteo de' Pasti*, &c. (Rothschild, Paris, 1883). M. Gustave Dreyfus's specimen of the medal of Christ is illustrated on pl. iii, 3, and described on p. 26. I have to thank the publisher for permitting me to reproduce the sketch in fig. 2 from this work. The specimen here reproduced (fig. 1) by kind permission of Mr. Henry Oppenheimer, is without a reverse.

no nimbus, and is turned to the right instead of to the left. It is, if anything, weaker in expression than the medallic head, which itself is quite the poorest of Pasti's productions. On the whole, we are justified in supposing that the drawing is a design by Pasti himself for his medal.

This work exercised comparatively little effect on the development of the medallic portraits of Christ. Its influence may, however, be traced in a repoussé silver medallion of the late fifteenth century in the Victoria and Albert Museum (fig. 3). This represents a head of Christ to l. with a cruciferous nimbus. The type is refined but weak, with a fairly long pointed beard, and long hair, a lock being brushed back from the forehead over the temple. The area of the nimbus is raised above the rest of the field ; its circle is of cable pattern. A metrical inscription in letters of late Gothic style runs round the bust : VIVA · DEI · FACIES · ET · SALVATORIS · IMAGO · Diameter, 63 mm.

In the collection of the late Don Pablo Bosch of Madrid is a large medal (fig. 4 *a*, *b*) which belongs to the same group :

Obv.—Bust of Christ to l., draped, otherwise as on fig. 3 ; across the field · I · N · · R · I · ; around, + RESPICE · IN · FACIEM · CHRISTI · TVI · SPECIOSVS · FORMA · PRE · FILIIS · HOMINVM (quatre-foils as stops, where visible).

Rev.—Incised inscription : + | VENITE · ADME : OM | NES · QVI LABORATIS ET | ONERATI ESTIS ET · EGORE | FICIAM · VOS · IVGVM · ENI | MEVMSVAVE · EST · ET | ONVS · MEVM · LEVE

Bronze gilt, 113 mm.[1] The lettering, especially on the reverse of this medal, is finely decorative, in the monumental style of about 1475. That is the time to which we may assign the origin of the medal, approximately. A specimen (obverse only), recently presented to the British Museum by Mr. E. G. Millar, shows the signature PHILIPI OPVS incised on the truncation of the bust.

The same type also occurs on a well-known *baiser de paix*,[2] of which the specimen in the Plaquette Room of the British Museum is illustrated here (fig. 5, 89 by 66 mm.). Christ is represented in profile to l., with cruciferous nimbus ; at the sides of the head, the letters I · N R · I ; above, the Holy Spirit between Sun and Moon. Molinier dates the piece to the end of the fifteenth

---

[1] I have to thank the late owner for the photographs from which the illustrations in the text are made.

[2] Molinier, *Les Plaquettes*, ii, p. 73, no. 461. Other specimens in the British Museum, at South Kensington, and at Berlin (Ital. Bronzes, 1305). M. Valton possessed a variety, now presumably in the Paris Cabinet, without the symbols above, and with INRI on a label below. Cf. Armand, *Les Médailleurs italiens*, iii, p. 149 *C*.

century. The way in which the bust is cut off is characteristic. The same type (apart from accessories) is exactly reproduced on a lead medallion (diameter, 100 mm.) found in the cemetery of Sainte-Livrade (Lot-et-Garonne).[1] The bust is flanked by the letters I N, and the field of the medallion decorated with

Fig. 4 a.—Medal in the Collection of the late Don Pablo Bosch.　*Obverse.*

incised ornaments. On the reverse is a Hebrew inscription, to which we shall return when dealing with the medals of the sixteenth century. M. de la Tour[2] thinks that this medallion is as late as the seventeenth century, and the work of an Italian artist. Although it reproduces a fifteenth-century type, there

---

[1] Published by M. G. Tholin, *Bull. de la Soc. Nat. des Antiquaires de France*, 1898, pp. 276 f.　　　　[2] *Bulletin de la Soc. Nat.*, p. 281.

is, I think, no doubt that it cannot be earlier than the second half of the sixteenth century.

It is interesting to note that Pasti's medal, or something very like it, was known to the painter Bartolommeo Montagna. In his altar-piece in the Brera, dated 1499, and representing the

Fig. 4 b.—Medal in the Collection of the late Don Pablo Bosch.   *Reverse*.

Madonna and four saints,[1] he has introduced two decorative medallions, of which one (fig. 6) seems to me to be suggested by the type of Pasti's medal. The medallions which are used thus by many painters from the second half of the fifteenth century onwards to decorate their architecture are not often, I believe, derived from modern medals, although, as in the case of actual

[1] T. Borenius, *The Painters of Vicenza*, p. 44.

architecture of the time, the influence of Roman coins is strong. But a careful examination of Italian paintings from this point of view might reveal some interesting features.

We now come to a much more important group of medals.[1] The chief peculiarities of the type of Christ on these medals are the retreating forehead, the thick fleshy nose and lips, the moustache which leaves the upper lip almost bare, starting from the wing of the nose, the short forked beard, the cruciferous nimbus with circles in the arms of the cross. The obverse inscription is, in one form or another, YHS XPC SALVA TOR MVNDI.

Fig. 5.—Plaquette in British Museum.

a. (Fig. 7).—𝑦HS in inscription ; stops, lozenges ; moustache on front of upper lip indicated ; field slightly sunk. *Rev.*—In wreath, inscription in fifteen lines :

PRESENTES | FIGVRE · AD · SIMILI | TVDINEM · DOMINIIHE| SV · SALVATORIS · NOSTRI | ET · APOSTOLI · PAVLI · IN · AMI| RALDO · IMPRESSE · PER · MAG| NI · THEVCRI · PREDECESSORES · AN | TIA · SINGVLARITER · OB- SERVA | TE · MISSE · SVNT · AB · IPSO · MAG | NO · THEVCRO · S · D · N · PAPE | INNOCENCIO · OCTAVO · PRO · SI | NGVLARI · CLENODIO · ADHV | NC EINEM · VT · SWM · FRA | TREM · CAPTIWM | RETINERET

[1] I may note, in passing, that all the medals of Christ of the fifteenth and earlier sixteenth centuries are undoubtedly cast, not struck. M. de Mély speaks (*Gaz. des Beaux-Arts*, 1898, tome xix, p. 490) as if some of them were struck. In view of the misapprehensions which prevail regarding the processes of medal-making, I may be excused for reminding my readers that the stages through which a cast medal passes are (*a*) the original model in relief, positive ; (*b*) the mould, hollow, negative, made by impressing *a* into moulding material ; (*c*) the cast from the mould, i.e. the complete medal. Further, it may be well to say a word as to the way in which varieties, such as those which are to be

Lettering, late Gothic; **N** is invariably reversed; stops, lozenges. For **ANTIA** and **EINEM** read **ANTEA** and **FINEM**. Bronze, 85 mm., Berlin.[1] Another specimen is in the Ashmolean Museum, Oxford (Fortnum Collection); a third at Milan (*Bull. de la Soc. des Ant. de l'Ouest*, 1889, p. 87); a fourth, apparently cast from, or else the original of, the Milan specimen, is in the Victoria and Albert Museum. It has the same breaks in the margin, and is pierced in exactly the same place. A fifth (83 mm.) with loop for suspension is in the British Museum; it reads **FINEM**, but is a poor cast.

A medallion cast from the obverse of a similar medal is inserted in a bell, cast in 1515 by Georgius Wagheuens, in the

Fig. 6.—Detail from Altar-piece by Montagna.

church of St. Olaus at Helsingør in Denmark. See F. Uldall, *Danmarks Middelalderlige Kirkeklokker* (Copenhagen, 1906),

described, came into existence. It was not necessary to build up an entirely new model. The artist could take an old medal and do one of two or three things. He could work on it with a graver, chasing and altering details, even cutting out one inscription and replacing it by another, or wholly modifying the bust. He could then make from this as many new casts as he pleased. Or, taking his old medal he could impress it in moulding material and make certain alterations at that stage; but it is doubtful whether much could be done in this way which could not more easily be effected by a third method. That was to make a wax cast, reproducing the old medal exactly, and then work on it as one pleased; this would then be the model from which the new variety could be cast. It is probable that not one of the varieties of the Salvator medal to be described was made from a new model, built up freehand in imitation of an original; the moulds were doubtless in all cases made mechanically from older specimens, and all specimens are the lineal descendants of one original.

[1] Dr. H. Dressel kindly sent me casts of this and the next medal.

Fig. 7.—Medal at Berlin.

pp. 303 f. This medal was also reproduced at Nancy, in the church of St. Èvre, on a bell cast in 1576, but now no longer existing.[1]

b. (Fig. 8).— · YH̄S · XP̄C in legend ; stops, pellets (two at the end). The field is roughened ; the area of the nimbus is sunk and filled with incised rays, the arms of the cross are also filled with incised lines. The whole medal is strongly tooled, especially

Fig. 8.—Medal at Berlin.

as regards the hair and the modelling of the face (note, e.g., the way in which the temple is sunk).

Rev.—In wreath, inscription as on preceding, with the following differences : at beginning, small cross ; stops, pellets ; AO for AD ; INPRESSE ; ANTEA ; SVMT ; DONO for CLENODIO ; FINEM ; RETINEAT.

Bronze, 84 mm., Berlin. Published by W. Bode, *Zeitschr. f. chr. Kunst*, 1888, pp. 347 f. ; cf. *Gaz. des Beaux-Arts*, 1898, vol. xix, p. 489.

The whole aspect of the lettering of this medal is somewhat earlier than that of *a* ; the D for instance is of a Gothic form ; the A has a more defined horizontal bar at the top. But the medal, to judge by the workmanship, has all the appearance of being a later modification of *a*. The artist, who realized that some people[2] might be

---

[1] *Bull. de la Soc. des Ant. de l'Ouest*, 1889, pp. 87 f.

[2] Such as Mgr. Barbier de Montault,

who in *Bull. de la Soc. des Ant. de l'Ouest*, 1889, p. 77, commits himself to the statement that the word has no meaning.

puzzled by the word **CLENODIO** (treasure, κλεινώδιον, cf. the German *Kleinod*), has replaced it by **DONO**.

c. (*Frontispiece*).—Stops, lozenges ; field slightly sunk ; circles in arms of cross ; the inscription, which is the same as on *a*, rests on an inner linear circle.

Rev.—Bust of St. Paul r., with long beard, wearing cloak fastened with bulla on r. shoulder ; plain circular nimbus ;

Fig. 9.—Medal in the Victoria and Albert Museum.

inscription : ·**PAVLVS· APOSTOLVS VAS· ELECTIONIS** ; before third word, small cross ; stops, lozenges ; field slightly sunk. The lettering is late Gothic, as on *a*.

Bronze, 83 mm., British Museum. A specimen, in some points better preserved than the Museum specimen, is in the possession of Sir Hercules Read.

A specimen in the Victoria and Albert Museum has, instead of the head of St. Paul, an engraved niello-like design of a tree with various flowers (pinks, marigolds, &c.). On the obverse (fig. 9) the field of the nimbus is decorated with punched annulets, and the background of the inscription is roughened. A second specimen, also at South Kensington, has short incised rays round the head and face.

d. (Fig. 10).—Inscription : **IHS · XPE**, &c. ; stops, inverted triangles ; field not sunk ; circles in arms of cross.

Rev.—In wreath, tied at bottom, inscription in six lines : **TV ES | CHRISTVS | FILIVS DEI VI | VI QVI INHVNC | MVNDVM VE | NISTI**.

Fig. 10.—Medal in the Ashmolean Museum.

Bronze, 91 mm., Ashmolean Museum, Oxford (Fortnum Collection).[1] Note (for future reference) that **INHVNC** is written as one word.   The lettering on both sides retains no Gothic elements.   A specimen (bronze gilt, 90 mm.) without reverse at Florence reads **XPC** on the obverse.[2]   For the legend, see St. John xi. 27.

e. (Fig. 11, obverse).—Head of St. Paul as on reverse of *c*, but of slightly later, softened style ; inscription : ·**PAVLVS APO-STOLVS   VAS ELECTIONIS** · ; stops, so far as preserved, inverted triangles.

Fig. 11.—Medal in the British Museum.

Rev.—In wreath, tied at bottom, inscription in seven lines : **BENEDICITE | IN EXCELSIS DEO | DOMINO DE FONTI | BVS ISRAEL IBI BENI | AMIM ADOLESCENTV | LVS IN MENTIS | EXCESSV.** In line 1 the letters **TE**, in line 5 **NTV**, are ligatured.

Bronze, 89 mm., British Museum.   The lettering on both sides of this medal is exactly the same as on *d*, with the same tendency to run words together, and there is no doubt that they are a pair.   For the legend see Ps. lxviii. 26, 27.

f. Obv. (Fig. 12).—Field not sunk ; circles in arms of cross ; inscription : **IESVS CHRISTVSSA LVATOR MVNDI** ; stops, obscure.

[1] I have to thank Mr. C. F. Bell for a cast of this medal.   It is mentioned by A. Way, *Archaeological Journal*, xxix (1872), p. 119.

[2] J. B. Supino, *Il Medagliere Mediceo*, p. 61, no. 125.   Professor Supino kindly sent me casts of this medal and of the Bargello specimen of *f*.

Rev.—Bust of a monk l. ; inscription : INQVIETV(M) · EST · COR MEVM · DONEC · REQVIESCAT · IN · TE ; stops, pellets (?).

Bronze, 45 mm., British Museum (from the Rome Sale, Sotheby's, 1904, no. 309). Another specimen at Florence (Supino, p. 191, no. 609). Cf. Armand, *Méd. ital.*, iii, p. 149 B. One at Berlin (*Amtliche Berichte*, 1911, p. 127). The quotation on the reverse is from St. Augustine, *Conf.* i. 1.

This medal is the work of a Florentine, about the year 1500 ; the portrait of the monk shows a good deal of power of characterization. It may well be by the same hand as the medal of Alberto Belli (who died in 1482) and as some of the medals of Savonarola. I have maintained elsewhere [1] that the portrait closely resembles the painting in the Academy at Florence of Dom Baltasar,

Fig. 12.—Medal in the British Museum.

Abbot of Vallombrosa, traditionally ascribed to Perugino, though some have named Raphael in connexion with it and its companion portrait of Dom Biagio, General of the Order of Vallombrosa.[2] Perugino may have painted the portraits about 1500. But I do not now feel convinced that the painting and the medal represent the same man.

g. Obv. (Fig. 13).—Bust of Christ, as on the previous medals, but the nimbus is removed from behind the head and indicated in profile at the top. Inscription : IĤS · XP̂C · SALVAT OR · MVNDI · Stops, apparently inverted triangles.

Rev.—Inscription in seven lines : IĤS · | XP̂S · DEVS | ET · HOMO · LA | PIS · ANGVLA | RIS · QVI · FECIT | VTRAQ · V | NVM, and around : ANIMAM · MEAM · PONO · PRO · OVIBVS · MEIS · Stops, usually inverted triangles.

[1] *Burlington Magazine*, January 1909, p. 215.
[2] Florence, Accademia, nos. 241–2 ;
Reinach, *Répert.* ii, p. 207 ; Crowe and Cavalcaselle, ed. Borenius, v, p. 308.

British Museum (presented by Mr. Max Rosenheim). Bronze, 38 mm. The circular inscription is from St. John x. 15 ; the other contains a reminiscence of Eph. ii. 14.

This last medal of Christ also had its companion medal of St. Paul (fig. 14) :

Obv.—Bust of St. Paul r., with long beard, wearing cloak fastened on r. shoulder with bulla ; no nimbus ; inscription : PAVLVS · DOCTOR GENTIVM

Rev.—Inscription in seven lines : PAVLVS · | RAPTVS · IN | PARADISVM | AVDIVIT · ARC | HANA · VERBA | QVE · N̄L · H̄O | I · LOQVI, and around : CHRISTO · CONFIXVS · SVM · CRVCI ·

Collection of Mr. Henry Oppenheimer, bronze gilt, 38 mm. (Lanna Catalogue 356, pl. 22). Another in the Collection of Signor Pio Santamaria. For the inscriptions see 2 Cor. xii. 4 and Gal. ii. 20.

Fig. 13.—Medal in the British Museum.

I do not know of any later medals with this type of Christ, which seems to have been superseded by the regular sixteenth-century type, which we shall deal with later. But some other small works reproduce the same type. One is a stone relief, about 70 cm. square, in the Museum of the Société des Antiquaires de l'Ouest at Poitiers (fig. 15). I reproduce it here from Père Gaffre's *Portraits du Christ* (p. 73).[1] It will be noticed that it reproduces exactly the type of the medal, but that the inscription has been transferred to a scroll and the abbreviations expanded as on *f*. The relief was found at Bignoux (Vienne), and appears to be French work of the early sixteenth century.

The medal also influenced German line-engravers and wood-cutters of the early sixteenth century. We have no less than four instances in point. The line-engraving (fig. 16), which seems

[1] By the author's kind permission. For further details I may refer to Mgr. Barbier de Montault's article in the *Bulletin de la Soc. des Antiquaires de l'Ouest*, 1889, p. 91.

to be the earliest of all these reproductions,[1] is at the same time the least skilful. Other works of the artist, who is known by the floriated A seen in the left-hand bottom corner of the illustration, have been described by Passavant and Lehrs ; [2] the latter authority dates his activity about 1500. For us the chief interest of the engraving lies in the fact, revealed by the text below, that it is taken from one of the earliest class of the medals with the long inscription referring to Bajazet's emerald on the reverse, and not, like Hans Burgkmair's woodcut, from the later variety with the short inscription TV ES CHRISTVS, &c. The character of the features is considerably altered, but the essentials of the type, except the fleshiness of the lips, are preserved. In the

Fig. 14.—Medal in the Collection of Mr. Henry Oppenheimer.

legend round the edge the engraving corresponds with the medal. Below is a short legend giving the substance of the long inscription on the original, viz. (abbreviations being resolved) : ' Imago et vera facies domini nostri iesu christi facta instar illius quam olim ingenti smaragdo impressam turcorum rex Innocentio papae octavo pro singulari clenodio misit.' Next comes an engraving dated 1507, published at Pforzheim ; [3] it represents the bust of Christ surrounded by a circle which obviously suggests the border of the medal. The nimbus is omitted. A finer work is that of Hans Burgkmair, about 1515, which I reproduce here (fig. 17).[4] This is admittedly and obviously a close copy of the

[1] My attention was called to this hitherto unpublished work, which is at Dresden, as well as to the woodcut described below, by Mr. Campbell Dodgson ; and for the photograph of the former I have to thank Professor Max Lehrs.

[2] Passavant, *Le Peintre Graveur*, ii, pp. 200 f. ; Lehrs, *Repert. f. Kunstwiss.*,

xii (1889), pp. 344 ff.

[3] Reproduced by L. Kaemmerer, *Hubert und Jan van Eyck*, p. 97.

[4] From a photograph obtained for me by Mr. Campbell Dodgson, who also called my attention to the engraving. I have omitted from the illustration the lettering above and below the design.

medal *d*, even to the use of the triangular stops. It will be noticed that the inscription of the reverse has been transferred to an outer circle, and that the copyist has slavishly followed the original in running the two words IN HVNC into one. Above the design is a long account in Latin of the supposed origin of the medal,

Fig. 15.—Stone Relief at Poitiers.
From Gaffre, Portr. du Christ.

to this effect : The portrait of Christ painted during his lifetime was perpetuated in a bronze and gold tablet of the fashion and size of this medal, faithfully reproducing the prototype. When the perfidious race of the Turks expelled the Christians from Asia, this holy effigy was hidden away. It is said on good authority that this bronze tablet, together with three gold coins bearing the same image, was found in the treasury of a certain king of the Turks, and was given by him to a certain noble German who was

Fig. 16.—German Engraving at Dresden.

on a visit to the Holy Sepulchre at Jerusalem. It was thus brought to Europe and copied by some painter. As a proof that this image represents the actual appearance of Christ, the letter of Lentulus is given below the engraving.

The reference to the copy made from the tablet by a painter is interesting in view of a point which we shall consider below.

The woodcut illustrated in fig. 18 comes from a work by Hans Sachs, published at Frankfurt in 1538 ;[1] the cuts are mostly by Beham, but that with which we are concerned seems

·H·B·

Fig. 17.—Engraving by Hans Burgkmair.

to be from another hand. The work has considerably less merit than its predecessors, but shows the persistence of the type in Germany. One may doubt whether it was taken directly from the medal, and not rather from some earlier woodcut.

The type of the medals is also reproduced with some alterations on a miniature published by Mgr. Barbier de Montault,[2]

[1] Hans Sachs, *Der Keiser, Kunige und anderer beder geschlecht personen kurtze Beschreibung*, &c. The head of Christ from which fig. 18 is taken is also repro-duced in Baer's *Frankfurter Bücherfreund*, 1900, nos. 9–11, p. 184.

[2] *Op. cit.*, p 116.

and dating from the seventeenth century. An inscription below says : Cette presente Figure est la representation et ressemblance de nostre Sauveur Jesus Christ gravee sur une Emeraude envoyee au Pape Paul V. par le Grand Turc, pour le rachapt d'une sienne qu'il tenoit pour lors prisonnière.[1]

But to discuss later reproductions of this kind would lead us into a consideration of the numerous later paintings, engravings,

Fig. 18.—German Woodcut of 1538.

&c., professing to reproduce the authentic portraits of Christ. For these I must refer to the articles by Messrs. C. W. King and Albert Way in the *Archaeological Journal*.[2] It is improbable that

[1] Thus, as we may see by comparison with the facts about Bajazet and his brother described below, Djem has changed his sex, Innocent VIII has become Paul V, and *retineret* has become *redimeret*—for so we can explain the origin of the idea that Bajazet wished to ransom the prisoner. Cf. ' redemption ', &c., in the pictures described by C. W. King, *Arch. Journ.* xxvii, pp. 181 f.

[2] xxvii (1870), pp. 181 f., and xxix (1872), pp. 109 f. See also the reprints in C. W. King's *Early Christian Numismatics*, &c. (1873). The tapestry panel referred to in the latter article, pp. 113 f., appears to be identical with that now in the British Museum. A small English panel exhibited by Mr. Clifford Smith at the Society of Antiquaries (*Proc. Soc. Ant.*, January 22, 1914) is among the most degraded of its class. In the text accompanying it Zizim has become ' Maximilian the Great ' ! Cp. also *Bodleian Quarterly Record*, iii (1920), no. 25.

any of the paintings described in these articles can be older than the sixteenth century.

A terracotta of Italian workmanship, acquired in Paris by M. Gaillard de la Dionnerie, is also said by Mgr. Barbier de Montault [1] to reproduce the type ; but it would appear from his description that the resemblance is not so exact as in the case of the French relief at Poitiers.

A bronze plaque at Berlin,[2] representing half figures of Christ and the Virgin, has also been brought into connexion with these medals. Although the heads are not in profile but nearly facing, the type of Christ is obviously the same. His right hand is raised in blessing, his left holds the cruciferous orb. The plaquette is a work of the ' school of Donatello ' of the second half of the fifteenth century.

In the Victoria and Albert Museum is a Limoges enamel (c. 1550) by J. Penicaud which is adapted from the Salvator medal ; it has the inscription IHS · XPC · SALVATOR · MVNDI · (stops, three-armed) up the left side and along the top of the panel.

What are we to make of the ' special picture of Christ cast in mould by Raphael de Urbino brought into England from Rome by Cardynall Poole ', which is mentioned in the inventory of Lumley Castle [3] drawn up in 1590 ? Possibly it was merely one of our ' Salvator ' medals.

For the sake of completeness I mention here another painting, although a reproduction is not forthcoming, and the original is inaccessible to me. It is a large miniature [4] in a New Testament in the library at Fulda, which has, unfortunately, been repainted in oils in the sixteenth century. It bears the inscription EFFIGIES · SALVATORIS · MVNDI · QVAE · ANTE · MVLTOS · ANNOS · EX · AEGIPTO · ARGENTINAM · TRANSMISSA · EST · RENOVATA · IAM · ANNO · 1588. It does not appear from Bode's description whether the picture exactly represents the profile type with which we are concerned.

But there is a representation of this type of the bust of Christ which is more important than any of the copies of the medal that we have discussed. It is a painting on an oak panel in the Kaiser Friedrich Museum at Berlin, representing Christ in the

[1] Op. cit., p. 106.
[2] Berlin, 997 ; Molinier, op. cit., ii, p. 73, no. 462 ; published by Bode, Ztschr. f. chr. Kunst, p. 350, and reproduced by Barbier de Montault, p. 72.
[3] E. Milner, Records of the Lumleys (1904), p. 333.
[4] Mentioned by Bode, Ztschr. f. chr. Kunst, 1888, p. 350.

act of blessing, the right hand being only partly seen (fig. 19).[1]
It used to be attributed to Jan van Eyck, who died in July 1441 ;
but Mr. Weale, the chief authority on the subject, considers it

Fig. 19.—Bust of Christ by a follower of Jan van Eyck.

to belong to the end of the fifteenth century. And, to be on the
safe side in the argument which ensues, we had better accept that
judgement. Thus a delicate and complicated question arises :

[1] No. 528 A ; ascribed in the official
catalogue (5th ed., 1904, p. 126) to an
imitator of Jan van Eyck. Bode, *op. cit.*,
pp. 347 f. ; Kaemmerer, *op. cit.*, p. 95 ;
W. H. J. Weale, *Hubert and John van Eyck*
(1908), p. 210 ; Weale and Brockwell,
The Van Eycks (1912), p. 188.

is the picture earlier or later than the medal (which as we shall see can hardly be earlier than 1492), the original source of the medal or inspired by it ; or do both go back to a common original ? The last is the view of Dr. von Bode. It will be observed that the picture is a fragment ; and he suggests that it once contained another person, probably the Virgin, as she is represented on the Berlin plaquette already described. Among the Limoges enamels from the Barwell Bequest in the British Museum is one representing busts of Christ (of the type in question) and of the Virgin, confronted, and evidently derived from some such picture as that of which half is preserved at Berlin.

Following the suggestion of the inscription on the reverse of the earliest variety of the medal, some, including Dr. von Bode, regard the type as an imitation of a Byzantine original. Let us reconsider that inscription. The medals *a* and *b*, it will have been noted, mention two ' figures ', of Jesus Christ and of the Apostle Paul, which were once ' impressed ', i.e. carved (in intaglio ?), on an emerald, which had been preserved with great care by the predecessors of the Grand Turk,[1] and sent by him to his Holiness Pope Innocent VIII [2] as an especial treasure, to the end that he might retain his brother in captivity.

Djem, or Zizim, defeated by his brother, the Sultan Bajazet II, fled to Egypt, and then appealed to the Knights of St. John at Rhodes, where he landed in 1482.[3] The Grand Master, who used him as a means of extorting money from Bajazet, sent him to France, whence he transferred him, in 1489, to Rome. There he lived a prisoner in the Vatican, the Pope receiving a heavy tribute from the Sultan on condition of keeping him in security. In 1492 Bajazet sent also the head of the sacred lance with which the side of Christ had been pierced. Djem died at Naples— perhaps poisoned—in 1495.

Now, if Bajazet sent the sacred lance-head, there is nothing improbable in the story that he sent the engraved emerald of which the presentation is recorded on our medals.[4] But no one, it would seem, has ever seen anything of the kind. Until the

---

[1] For *Theucer* = Turk in the fifteenth century see Ducange *s.v. Teucri.*

[2] Von Bode remarks that the inscription shows the medal to have been made during Innocent's occupation of the Papal chair (1484–92). This is probable, but the inscription hardly proves it.

[3] For the story of this prince see Gregorovius, *Gesch. der Stadt Rom*, vii, pp. 290 ff., 374 (Eng. ed., pp. 305 ff., 394).

[4] Mgr. de Montault's reasons (p. 118) for doubting that the emerald ever existed are insufficient.

Treasury of St. Peter's yields up its secrets, we must proceed on the assumption that the emerald, if it was ever in the possession of the Vatican, has disappeared. Two portraits are spoken of, but it seems to be implied that they were on the same stone. A head of Christ engraved on a precious stone appears to have been among the treasures at St. Sophia as early as the tenth century. As M. de Mély has pointed out,[1] Anthony of Novgorod, describing the treasures of Constantinople in A.D. 1200, says that he saw a large silver dish, used for Divine service, which was given by Olga, the Russian grand duchess, to the Patriarch ; in which dish is a precious stone, with the effigy of Christ chased thereon, from which impressions are taken.[2] As Olga died in 968, this stone must have been as old as the tenth century.

Possibly, then, the emerald sent by Bajazet to Rome in or about 1492 was at least as old as the tenth century, being identical with Olga's. But then, what of the head of St. Paul ?

M. de Mély, in calling attention to the passage from the Russian pilgrim, maintains that in the Christ-type of the medal we have a specimen—modified no doubt by the hand of the Renaissance artist, but still representing the original—of Byzantine glyptic art of the tenth century. Dr. von Bode,[3] also,

---

[1] *Gazette des Beaux-Arts*, 1898, tome xix, p. 492.

[2] Antonius Novgorodensis, *Liber qui dicitur Peregrinus*. Latin version of extracts in P. E. D. Riant, *Exuviae*, ii (1878), p. 219 : ' Discus sacrificii magnus argenteus, ab Olga Russica, magna ducissa, quae illum donavit pontifici in usus sacrificii, quando in caesaream urbem venit, ut baptizaretur. . . . In disco illo Olgae lapis quidam pretiosus est, coelatam exhibens Christi effigiem, cuius signacula impressa desumuntur ad quasvis gratias obtinendas ; desuper autem discus margaritis ornatus est.' [Another version for *magna . . . bapt.* gives *donatus, quae C. P. ad tributum percipiendum venerat.*]

[3] This critic's latest handling of the matter is worth considering. He writes (*Amtliche Berichte aus den königlichen Kunstsammlungen*, March 1911, p. 127) that the profile of Christ (on the reverse of a medal with a monk's head, similar to our fig. 12) is imitated from the known ancient Byzantine cameo in the Treasury of St. Peter's (' dem bekannten altbyzantinischen Kameo im Schatz der Peterskirche nachgebildet ist '). He goes on to point out that in relief and handling the head of the monk resembles the heads of Savonarola and his supporters and opponents, which he (Dr. von Bode) has sought to show to be the work of Niccolò (di) Forzore. Since the head of Christ on the reverse exactly resembles the known larger plaquette (imitated from the said Byzantine cameo), to which there is a companion piece with a head of St. Peter, it is probable, he concludes, that these two plaquettes are also works of Niccolò Fiorentino. This passage contains some details of a most surprising kind. If the description of the cameo as ' known ' means anything more than that it has been talked of for centuries, without any serious evidence of its character or appearance, or even of its

assumes that the medal-type is a faithful copy of the head on the emerald, and suggests that copies of the famous stone found their way to the West long before the emerald itself came to Rome. This last suggestion is certainly borne out by the remark of Anthony that *signacula impressa desumuntur ad quasvis gratias*

existence at the present time, being produced, Dr. von Bode ought to have been more precise. He may, for all we know, have had that access to some of the treasures of St. Peter's which is denied to less fortunate investigators ; but he has never, it would seem, made his discovery public. We are therefore forced to assume that he knows no more about the ' known ' Byzantine cameo than any one else. He goes on to speak of ' plaquettes ' of Christ and St. Peter, companion pieces. The standard works on plaquettes record none such. It is probable that he means to refer to specimens of the medal of Christ which have been cast without reverses. To call such pieces plaquettes is merely misleading. But, letting that pass, what are we to make of the companion piece with the head of St. Peter ? Neither among plaquettes nor medals is it possible to find any work in any way answering to that description. Has Dr. von Bode again special knowledge, which he does not choose to divulge, or is he merely confusing St. Peter with St. Paul ? If we must decide, the balance of probability seems to incline to the latter alternative. There are other matters in the official report from which the above passage is taken, which seem to indicate that carelessness of thought and method are at the bottom of the mystery. Amongst the acquisitions of the Berlin Museum, which the Director illustrates and describes, are two medallic pieces, the one a portrait of the painter Francia, the other a design of Hercules and Atlas with the globe, with the inscription ' Hi duo, ille solus '. The Francia is described as a leaden model for a medal which was never carried out or is unknown. To those who are in the least

familiar with the history of medallic art, it should be at once obvious that it is a grotesque forgery. It belongs to a class, including medals of Primaticcio and Guercino, which were made by some bungling hand, hardly earlier than 1650. (All three are illustrated together in my *Portrait Medals of Italian Artists of the Renaissance*, pl. XXXII.) Of the Hercules and Atlas design Dr. von Bode writes that it is without doubt the reverse of an unknown or never executed medal, of which the broad, large handling of form betrays an artist of the character of Leone Leoni (' deren breite, grosszügige Formenbehandlung einen Künstler in der Art des Leone Leoni verrät '). Again those dangerous words ' unknown or never carried out ' ! This wonderful design, which to the Director of the Prussian Museums is the work of an Italian artist such as Leone Leoni, is nothing but the reverse of a medal by a French artist of the seventeenth century, representing Cardinal Mazarin, which he might have found illustrated in its complete form by reference to so well known a work as the *Trésor de Numismatique* (Médailles françaises, i, pl. LXVI, 5). But even were the design otherwise unknown, the lettering alone is enough to betray it. It has seemed desirable to dwell upon these matters, hardly in themselves relevant to the subject of this book, because they throw some light on the quality of Dr. von Bode's expertise in regard to medallic art, and justify us in refusing to accept without careful discrimination his views on the origin of the medal of Christ. The criticism of medals requires special training, and cannot be regarded as a trifle which any critic of sculpture can dispatch in his spare time.

obtinendas; whatever exactly this may mean, it is clear that impressions of the gem were made.

The whole question may, however, be approached from another point of view ; and we may clear the way by asking whether, so far as our knowledge of Byzantine art goes, there is anything which bears the least resemblance to the type of the Flemish picture and the medals. I believe that every Byzantinist will answer in the negative.[1] On the other hand, the type in the Flemish picture has all the appearance of being taken straight from life ;[2] there is nothing Byzantine about it ; and although it corresponds with the literary tradition so far as concerns the beard and hair, there is absolutely nothing in the head which suggests a hieratic artistic tradition.

Further, there is, I think, no doubt that the type of face is characteristic of Flemish art in the fifteenth century. Even in full-face representations, one is able to recognize the thick, fleshy lips and nose, with the moustache starting from the corners of the upper lip, in paintings and in illuminated manuscripts from the time of Jan van Eyck down to the early sixteenth century ; and when in profile, one sees also the retreating forehead. It is important to note that features such as this are given not only to Christ, but also to any face to which it is desired to assign prominence.[3] On the other hand, it is extremely rare to find any approximation to the type in art south of the

---

[1] It is quite possible that Olga's emerald reproduced the Edessa portrait which was translated to Constantinople in 944 (see v. Dobschütz, *Christusbilder*, 1899, pp. 149 ff.). In this case it would be a facing head. The profile treatment would be almost an anomaly in Byzantine art. The facing bust on the cameo in the Bibliothèque Nationale (Babelon, *Camées* 333, pl. xxxix) shows the typical Byzantine treatment, but I cannot agree with M. de Mély (*Gaz. des Beaux-Arts*, 1898, vol. xix, p. 492) that this resembles the type which we find in profile on our medals.

[2] It is only fair to note that Kaemmerer (p. 101) says that the picture is probably not the result of direct study from the life, but a copy of the so-called *vera effigies*. I simply cannot agree.

[3] I note here some of the Dutch, Flemish, or North French MSS. in the British Museum, which it is instructive to compare. 17267 (Dutch, early or middle of saec. xv), fol. 28 b, 42 b ; Sloane 2471 (Flemish illuminations, second third of saec. xv), fol. 54 b ; 35313 (late xv), fol. 8, 21, 22 b, 222 b ; 18851 (late xv), fol. 77, 345 b ; 17280 (Flemish, late xv), fol. 202 b, 221 b. The type is very prominent throughout the fifteenth century in the Netherland school of painting ; for late instances see the works of Hieronymus Bosch and Jan Mostaert, illustrated in M. Friedländer, *Meisterwerke der niederl. Malerei*, pls. 84, 85, 86. It would not be difficult to cite instances from English fifteenth-century art, such as the alabaster reliefs of the Nottingham school.

Alps,[1] and no one has yet produced a parallel to it from Byzantine art.

If therefore we have no definite instance of the occurrence of the type in question in Byzantine art ; if it occurs in a Flemish picture of the fifteenth century, and a similar treatment of hair and features is characteristic of Flemish art, while only exceptionally found south of the Alps, down to the sixteenth century—how can we avoid the conclusion that the statement connecting the medals with Bajazet's emerald must be regarded with suspicion ?

The inscription says that there were two heads, one of Christ, the other of St. Paul. Mgr. de Montault has suggested (p. 79) that two medals were made, one representing each head, but with the same inscription mentioning both : PRESENTES FIGVRE, &c. Such a medal of St. Paul we do not actually possess ; but the medal *c* shows that a head of St. Paul was connected with the head of Christ, supposed to be copied from the emerald. If the Christ reproduces the type of the emerald, we are justified in supposing that the St Paul does the same. And that is a *reductio ad absurdum* ; for I do not think that any one, even if he believe in the Byzantine origin of the former, will fail to recognize a pure Italian type in the latter.

We infer, therefore, that the inscription on the reverse of the early medals *a*, *b* is a pious fiction, intended to give currency to the portrait on the obverse by assigning to it a respectable pedigree. The artists of the period were no more conscientious in such matters than their successors of the sixteenth and seven-

---

[1] Instances I have noted are in the Brit. Mus. MS. 15265 (saec. xiv) and in the Veronese fresco (second half of saec. xv) over the main entrance to San Fermo Maggiore, in which the face of St. Longinus bears some slight resemblance to the type. Northern influence was strong in Verona. A good instance, more or less contemporary with the medal, is in the Book of Hours of Bona Sforza (Brit. Mus. MS. 34294, as in fol. 88, reproduced in Warner, *Reprod. from Illum. MSS.*, ser. iii, 1908, pl. xlii). It should be noted that, although this illumination is ascribed to an Italian hand, many of the illuminations in the same book are Flemish, and Flemish influence on the Italian illuminator need not surprise us. There is some approximation to the type also in Verrocchio's Christ in the famous group (finished in 1480) on the outside of Or San Michele ; indeed I have heard that, on the strength of the resemblance, the medal with which we are dealing has been attributed to the great sculptor. It is quite unworthy of him from the point of view of technique. The peculiar treatment of the moustache is in itself not confined to the North ; thus we find it in the Santo Volto of Lucca (Gaffre, *Les Portraits du Christ*, pl. xviii).

teenth centuries, who would not scruple to describe a fancy head of Christ as a faithful copy of the emerald of Bajazet.[1]

We may conclude, therefore, as regards the relation between the picture and the medal, that either the medal is copied from the picture, or, if they have a common origin, that origin is to be sought in a Flemish painting approximating to the extant picture, and not in any way dependent on a Byzantine model.

The medal has been briefly discussed by the late Natalis Rondot in his posthumous work on French medallists and coin engravers.[2] A certain number of specimens, he states, have been met with at Lyon. In 1517 the échevins of that city presented a specimen in gold to the wife of the General of Finance of Languedoc. De Longpérier (presumably Adrien of that name) possessed a fine specimen in yellow bronze which he regarded as of Lyonnese origin. This attribution M. Rondot regards as possible. The medal, he says, is certainly French ; but this statement he qualifies by the addition that, to judge by the heads and the character of the lettering, it must be a French reproduction, made in the first years of the sixteenth century, of an Italian piece of the end of the fifteenth.

To distinguish between an Italian original of the end of the fifteenth century and a French reproduction made a few years later by the casting process, and possibly differing only in the character of the lettering—note that the busts in the various extant specimens differ in no essential characteristics—is a process of considerable delicacy. It is still more delicate when the whole question is complicated by the fact that the more remarkable of the two heads is derived from a painting by a Northern master. Unfortunately very little is known of French work of that date which can be compared with the medal. But, as Sir Hercules Read points out to me, an important monument of the potter's art at Lyon in the early sixteenth century is the tile (fig. 20) with the head of St. John the Baptist, presented to the British Museum by Major-General Meyrick.[3] As to this, Mr. Solon remarks that the modelling of the head is absolutely French in style. There may be a superficial resemblance between this head and the head of Christ on our medals ; but it is hardly

[1] Cf. C. W. King, in *Archaeological Journal*, xxvii (1870), p. 181.

[2] *Les Médailleurs et les Graveurs de Monnaies Jetons et Médailles en France*, ed. by H. de la Tour (Paris, 1904), p. 83.

[3] M. L. Solon, *Hist. and Descr. of the Old French Faience* (1903), fig. 4.

enough to justify any argument as to community of origin. In any case we have to remember two things. First, that Italian influence was exceedingly strong at Lyon at the time. As

Fig. 20.—Tile with head of St. John Baptist. British Museum.

Mr. Solon remarks (p. 41), ' of the twenty-seven master potters known to have been at work at Lyon in the early part of the sixteenth century, seven were of Italian origin ; they are said to have practised their art after the fashion used in their own country'. Second, that the resemblance between the medal and the terra-cotta is confined to the head of Christ on the former ; the treatment of the head of St. Paul is absolutely different. In other words, it is a resemblance of type rather than of style. And this resemblance of type may be due to the influence of some Northern model on the designer of the tile. One would like to have had more explicit reasons for Rondot's opinion. At present (assuming him to admit the derivation of the head of Christ from the Flemish painting) we find him committed to the view that we have a French imitation (early sixteenth century) of a lost Italian medal (late fifteenth century), of which one side was copied from a Flemish painting (late fifteenth century) and the other was of Italian origin (presumably contemporary). I prefer to take refuge in the less subtle and romantic theory that the Italian medal is not lost but is to be found in some at least of the many varieties in which the medal with the two heads exists.[1]

The medals are of Italian origin. We have nothing in the early medallic art of the Netherlands, or of any other country, to warrant our ascribing the medal *a* to any part of the world save Italy. It is well known that early Flemish pictures found their way into Italian collections ;[2] and there is no difficulty therefore in supposing that the picture now at Berlin, or an earlier version of it, was known to the Italian artist who invented the medal with which we are concerned. But, not possessing any such model for his St. Paul, he produced a head of purely Italian type. This explains the different feeling which characterizes the two heads, and which gives the impression that the medal *c* is a hybrid, i.e. a combination of two obverses which do not belong to each other. From some medal combining the two heads, as in *c*, a later artist, who was unaware of the medals with the inscription attributing the origin of the type to the emerald, made the two medals *d* and *e*, to which he attached new reverse inscriptions. All this happened probably after 1492 (when Bajazet sent the lance-head and, perhaps, also the emerald) and before 1507, the date of the Pforzheim engraving, or, if that is taken from the earlier medal, before about 1515, to which time Burgkmair's engraving probably belongs. The statement

---

[1] In the British Museum is a specimen, presented by the late Mr. Max Rosenheim, in which the head of Christ is surrounded by fine incised rays.

[2] See Jacques Mesnil, *L'Art au Nord et au Sud des Alpes* (1911), especially p. 20, on the devotional aspect of the Northern pictures.

on Burgkmair's sheet, to the effect that the original portraits of Christ were copied by a painter, I take to reveal the fact that the connexion between this type and the Flemish painting was known.

Admitting that the medal is of Italian origin, can we be more precise, and indicate the school to which it belongs ? Those who are familiar with the products of the Italian schools of the end of the fifteenth century will not fail to recognize, in the handling of the bust and the hair, traces of the Florentine manner. So much, indeed, of the ordinary journeyman work of the Florentines has been attributed to the chief master of that school, Niccolò di Forzore Spinelli, that it would be strange if these Christ medals had escaped. But Dr. von Bode, as we have seen, has not hesitated to annex them for his favourite. They have also, as I have indicated above (p. 36, note 1), been assigned to an even greater Florentine, Verrocchio, on what appear to me to be inadequate grounds. But Florentine influence was strong in Rome also at the end of the century, and I am inclined to suggest that the medal was made, so to speak, in the shadow of the Vatican, where the treasure, which it falsely professed to reproduce, was laid up. There is something of the classicizing spirit in the style of the head of St. Paul, in particular, which suggests Rome rather than Florence.

The genealogy of the type may therefore be expressed as follows :

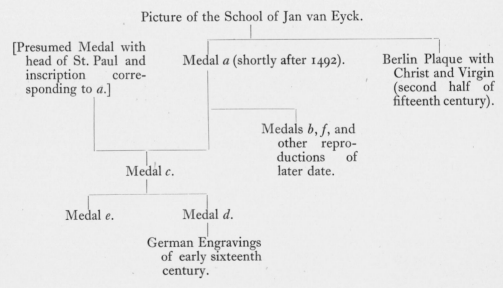

Picture of the School of Jan van Eyck.

[Presumed Medal with head of St. Paul and inscription corresponding to a.]

Medal a (shortly after 1492).

Berlin Plaque with Christ and Virgin (second half of fifteenth century).

Medals b, f, and other reproductions of later date.

Medal c.

Medal e.   Medal d.

German Engravings of early sixteenth century.

This theory of the history of the type appears to me, due account being taken of the psychology of fifteenth-century artists, to make legitimate use of our data.   As I have said, there is no reason to doubt that there was an actual antique emerald sent from Constantinople by Bajazet to the Vatican.   But whom the heads on it actually represented is another question ; and further, when we come to the claim of the medals to represent that gem, our suspicions are aroused, and investigation becomes necessary.

There is, however, an alternative theory in explanation of the real origin of the two heads of Christ and St. Paul, which Sir Martin Conway has put before me, and kindly allows me to reproduce ; I do so as far as possible in his own words :

The statement that there were two heads engraved upon the emerald is very suggestive, and at once recalls the third- and fourth-century gems with double heads, and other decorative objects thus treated.   For example, a marriage-ring in the Berlin Museum,[1] with two bust portraits in profile confronted ; or the fifth-century ring in the British Museum ; [2] and plenty more might be cited.[3]   In Berlin [4] is a little gold encolpion of the fourth century, from Egypt, with two such confronted heads in profile of SS. Peter and Paul.   Such confronted profiles of the two saints with the chi-rho monogram between them adorn a bronze repoussé plaque [5] and also appear on gold-glass ; [6] and there is also a single head of the type (called Peter) in the Basilewsky Collection.[7]

Now the statement that the gem was engraved with the heads of Christ and St. Paul seems to suggest that it was in reality a third- to fourth-century gem with the heads of Peter and Paul. The head of Paul in fig. 11 perfectly corresponds with the above cited examples.   The head of Christ, however, differs in having long hair, whereas both the Apostles in all the examples cited have short hair ; but the form of beard is the same.[8]

[1] *Amtliche Berichte*, November 1913, p. 34.

[2] Dalton, *Catalogue of the Finger Rings*, no. 127 ; *Catalogue of Early Christian Antiquities*, no. 207.

[3] e. g. *Proc. Soc. Ant.* xxii. 101.

[4] Wulff, *Altchr. &c. Bildwerke*, 1118.

[5] *Bull. d'Archeol. Crist.*, 1887, p. 130, pl. X, 3 (found in the Catacomb of S. Agnese).   Compare the similar bronze in the Vatican Library Museum, *ibid.*, pl. X, 2.

[6] Deville, *Hist. de l'Art de la Verrerie*, 1873, pl. 29 B.

[7] Darcel et Basilewsky, *Coll. Basilewsky*, pl. V.

[8] It is to be noted that on the well-known disc from the cemetery of Domitilla (*Bullett.*, *loc. cit.*, pl. X, 1) the beards are short and round.

There may then have been a real gem at the Vatican, on a tiny scale, engraved with heads of Peter and Paul, but without their names. There may have been, as in some such representations we know there was, a small star or cross or chi-rho monogram between the two heads, which may have been taken to identify one of the heads as Christ. Some artist, being told that the heads were Christ and Paul, may have made a painted copy of it on a large scale, giving it of course his own local style and making the Christ long-haired. This artist may have been Flemish, and have worked from a wax impression. Granted that the Berlin picture is the first so painted, and that it ever had both heads, the introduction of a blessing hand was the only way in which the presence of two heads of equal dimensions and importance could be explained and a proper predominance given to Christ's head.

The mistake has been in looking for the original in Byzantine days. It would seem that these confronted busts are a pre-Byzantine type. Of course the treasury at Constantinople may have contained many objects brought from Rome or made in any and every part of the Empire; there is, therefore, no inherent improbability in the statement that the gem was sent from Constantinople.

This is Sir Martin Conway's theory, and it presents remarkable attractions. It may have already occurred to the reader that the original juxtaposition of Christ and St. Paul in the form presumed seems a little hard to explain. One might expect to find Christ between two other persons; but why should St. Paul have been chosen to be placed alone with his Master on a gem? On the other hand, the confronted heads of SS. Peter and Paul were the obvious thing. Again, an artist familiar with the later conception of St. Peter, as it is found, for instance, on mediaeval Papal bullae, may well have failed to recognize the long-bearded type as it is seen on the bronze of S. Agnese, and may have taken it for Christ. It may be noted that on the fifteenth-century medals the heads of Christ and St. Paul face to left and right respectively; it may therefore be assumed that if they were both copied from some one design, on that original they were confronted. All this is in favour of Sir Martin's theory.

If I point out one or two objections to it, it is not because it conflicts with my own view, which is only concerned with denying the direct Byzantine origin of the Christ-type on our medal. We know that there existed a design of some kind with the two busts of Christ, blessing, and the Virgin ; the Berlin plaquette and the Barwell enamel [1] are enough to prove that ; and in both these the type of Christ is akin to that on the medal and in the Berlin picture. It seems only reasonable to assume that the Berlin picture when complete contained not St. Paul as the second figure but the Virgin. Secondly, why should the artist, copying the supposed early gem, have so thoroughly transformed the one head not merely by giving it the long hair which he supposed to be characteristic of Christ, but also by making it wholly Flemish in feeling, while he succeeded in retaining the classical Roman type for his St. Paul ? Is it not more likely that the ultimate source of the medal of Christ was one thing (the Flemish picture), and that of the medal of Paul another ?

Whatever be the solution, it is to be repeated that Sir Martin's theory and my own are not incompatible. My theory assumes that the head of Christ on the medal was derived from a Flemish picture ; his explains the origin of that picture.

II. The Sixteenth Century

WITH the sixteenth century the medallic type of Christ assumes a character very different from that which we have met with in the late quattrocento. Here again, though much less directly than in the former case, the medallic type was inspired by a great painter. We shall see that the theory which connects it directly with no less an artist than Leonardo da Vinci cannot be regarded as tenable. Since Leonardo practically dominated the whole of North Italian art in his time, it is clear that but for him the medallic type as we know it would not have come into existence ; but the filiation with him is not direct.

Among the engravings of Raphael Morghen is a medallion representing the draped bust of Christ to the left, without nimbus, but with a cross at the back of the head ; the beard is short, the hair long and flowing. Around is the inscription :
· XPS · REX · VENIT · IN · PACE · ET · DEVS · HOMO · FACTVS · EST · ✠ ·

---

[1] The panels of Christ and the Virgin by Quentin Metsys, in the National Gallery and elsewhere, are a free development of a similar scheme.

Below we read : *L'Originale d'egual grandezza creduto di Leonardo, trovasi nella Galleria de' Fratelli Trivulzio a Milano.*

Fig. 21.—Miniature in the Trivulzio Collection, Milan.

The original in question is here reproduced (fig. 21) by the kind permission of its owner, the Prince Trivulzio.[1]

That it is by Leonardo it would be extremely rash to assert ;

[1] I have also to thank the late M. H. de la Tour, of the Cabinet des Médailles, Bibliothèque Nationale, for the photograph from which the illustration is made, and for generously allowing me to anticipate his publication of it. He first called attention to its bearing on the subject in *Bull. de la Soc. des Ant. de Fr.*, 1898, p. 385. He there also mentions a silverpoint drawing in the British Museum attributed to Leonardo, as resembling the head on the medals with which we have to deal. The drawing, however, cannot be by Leonardo ; apart from the question of its style, it is dated (in the top left-hand corner) 1532 ; and after a careful examination of it I am bound to say that its resemblance to the head on the medals seems to me to be very slight.

I do not find it assigned to him in any authoritative book on his work, and to more than one student of that painter Luinesque, rather than Leonardesque, seems to be the epithet most proper to describe its somewhat sweet effeminate beauty.

The medal which presents exactly the same type, and which I shall henceforward call, for convenience' sake, the XPS · REX medal, is fairly common, and is found with more than one reverse. It is unnecessary to describe the obverse of these pieces again ; the three reverses which are known to me are—

(1) The YHS trigram in a glory of flames (i.e. the symbol

Fig. 22.—Medal in Mr. Maurice Rosenheim's Collection.

especially associated with San Bernardino of Siena) ; around, YHS · XPS · OPTIMVS · MAXIMVS · SALVVM · ME · FAC :

Mr. Maurice Rosenheim's Collection. Bronze, cast, 47·5 mm. (fig. 22).
British Museum. Bronze, cast, 47 mm.
The letters of the YHS monogram are of Gothic form, the hasta of the h being crossed. In the inscription only the Y is of Gothic form ; a small cross rests on the bar of the H ; the first V of SALVVM is inserted ; and the letters ME are ligatured.

(2) The dead Christ lying on the knees of the Virgin, who is seated before the cross ; on the left, a nimbate disciple supports the head of Christ ; to the right stands the Magdalen tearing her hair. Around, a wreath.

British Museum. Bronze, cast, 46 mm. (fig. 23).
Parma. 46 mm. Armand, iii, p. 149 D.

(3) A Hebrew inscription, with which we shall deal later.

Bronze, 44 mm. Published by L. Germain, *Bull. de la Soc. Nat. des Ant. de France*, 1898, p. 387, and *Rev. de l'Art chrétien*, 1900, p. 424.

It should be observed that this third reverse was not made specially for the obverse, but, as is clear from its smaller size, was simply cast on from a specimen of the 'Hebrew medal' discussed later. It is evident enough from M. Germain's illustration that his medal is a surmoulage or after-cast, and that he cannot argue from the conjunction of the two sides that the Latin and the Hebrew inscriptions mean the same thing, although that is in itself likely.

Fig. 23.
Medal in the British Museum.

At first sight one hardly considers the possibility that the Trivulzio miniature may itself be not an original. Such a possibility must, however, be taken into account for more than one reason. We know that from the latter half of the fifteenth century onwards it was the custom to copy medals in miniatures. The most striking instance is perhaps that furnished by the reproduction on the title-page of a manuscript in the Laurentiana, of a medal of Cosimo de' Medici the Elder.[1] Another good instance is the copy of the reverse of Pisanello's 'Liberalitas' medal of Alfonso of Aragon on the first title-page of Andr. Contrarius's 'Defence of Plato'.[2] Now the composition of the Trivulzio miniature is entirely medallic in character : witness the arrangement of the legend on a circular border which is broken by the front of the bust. The use of the triangular stops also points to a

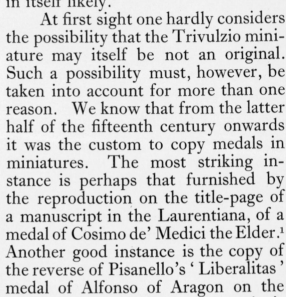

Fig. 24.—From Rouille,
Promptuaire des Médailles.

medallic original ; we have noticed the frequent occurrence of these stops in the fifteenth-century medals. At the same time it must be confessed that the extant medals of this type all have ordinary stops ; so that if the miniature was copied from a medal, that particular medal has disappeared.

One of the earliest printed numismatic books is the *Promp-*

---

[1] See Müntz, *Les Précurseurs,* pp. 156, 158.

[2] Bibl. Nat., MS. Lat. 12947 (Stevenson, *Mél. de l'École française,* viii, pp. 470 f., where other instances are given). A reproduction facing p. 424 of Müntz, *Ren. à l'époque de Charles VIII.*

tuaire des Médailles of Guillaume Rouille, the drawings for which were done by the artist Corneille de la Haye. Editions in French, Latin, Spanish, and Italian were printed in the same year, 1553. On p. 9 of the second part we find (see fig. 24) a medal of Christ which reproduces the same type, and is evidently derived from an actual medal.[1] The bust is to the right, not, as in the medals with which we have dealt so far, to the left; and this is probably due to the artist's having engraved the bust as he saw it on the medal to the left, forgetting that it would be reversed in printing. That the original medal was somewhat worn is shown by the treatment of the drapery on the right shoulder, where two folds have run together owing to wearing away of the edges. No reverse is shown; but in the field is the name ' Jesus ' in Hebrew letters (with points), and around is the inscription CHRISTVS REX VENIT IN PACE DEVS HOMO FACTVS EST. The halo consists of rays arranged in a square with incurved sides, suggesting a cross.

This engraving is obviously modelled on the XPS · REX medal, which must therefore have been in existence some time earlier.

This brings us to a group of medals which have been the subject of considerable controversy, a group which includes the commonest of all medals of Christ, and which, from the fact that the inscriptions on them are all in Hebrew, we may call the Hebrew group.[2] The earliest literary mention of medals of this kind dates from 1538.

Theseus Ambrosius Albonesius, in a book published in 1539,[3] speaks of the forms of the ' Samaritan ' letters used by coin-engravers in their inscriptions, such ' as, when I was at Rome in the happier days of Pope Julius II, and in the time of Leo X his successor, I remember to have seen on bronze coins; and last year an image of our Saviour cast in bronze, with Samaritan

---

[1] It is not superfluous to say this, because many of the ' medals ' reproduced in this book are pure inventions of the artist.

[2] In dealing with this group I have had the kind assistance of my colleague Dr. L. D. Barnett, without which I should have hesitated to make any decided statements about questions of interpretation of the Hebrew inscriptions. The most recent discussions of these medals are by S. Ferarès, *Les Médailles du Christ*

à légendes hébraïques de la Bibliothèque Nationale, in *Rev. Num.*, 1917, pp. 269–79, with a plate illustrating seven examples, belonging to the varieties illustrated in figs. 24 and 26; and by L. Germain, in *Rev. Num.*, 1919, pp. 89–94.

[3] *Introductio in Chaldaicam linguam, Syriacam, atque Armenicam, et decem alias linguas* (Pavia, 1539), fol. 21 verso ff.

letters, was shown to me by a lady, of most holy reputation, whose name (lest I offend her most chaste ears) I will wrap in silence, when she was passing through Ferrara, and was travelling by boat along the Po to Venice ; on the other side of which coin were to be seen letters cast or struck, of which the sense was as follows : Messiah the King came in peace, God became man, or incarnate '.[1]

The subsequent literature of the medal of Christ is enormous. It seems almost criminal to add to it ; but a sober re-statement of the problem seems to be required. The discussion of attempts to disentangle the meaning of a Hebrew inscription which is either blundered or wilfully distorted presents few attractions except to philologists. The general reader, therefore, who has struggled to this point, may be wise if he skips the following pages, and rests content with the verdict of the excellent Jobert, who, at the end of the seventeenth century, gave a correct estimate of the age of the medal in these words : [2] ' Ainsi la Medaille de Jesus-Christ quoy qu'elle eût pû estre faite par quelque Juif converti au Christianisme, est cependant une de ces Medailles faites à plaisir dans les derniers siecles, & dont les curieux ne doivent faire aucun estat.'

It is difficult to guess what were the bronze coins which Albonesius once saw in Rome in the time of Julius II (1503–13) or Leo X (1513–21). But of medals with the image of Christ with Hebrew lettering we have a choice of four or five kinds in our attempt to identify what he describes. Hitherto attempts at such identification have not been very plausible ; nothing that was known to have survived seemed to come very near to the sense of the inscription as rendered by Albonesius. Recently, however, a very roughly cast medal (Fig. 25) has come to light, differing slightly but decidedly from all others of the Hebrew group, which I think may be like the piece which the old scholar saw :

(1) *Obv.*—Bust of Christ l., in high relief, with a cross behind the head, and in front the square Hebrew letters אי״ש ל

---

[1] *Messias rex venit in pace, Deus homo factus est, vel incarnatus est.*

[2] *La Science des Médailles*, Amsterdam, 1693, p. 129. Because the author in the preceding passage speaks of false coins of the Jews, struck, not many years before he wrote, in Germany, he has been taken to say that the medal of Christ was itself made in Germany. But his words will not, I think, bear that interpretation ; all that he means is that the medal is of relatively modern origin.

Rev.—Inscription in good square Hebrew lettering,

משיח | מלך בא בש|ולום, ואדם אל|, רם עשוי | חי

Fig. 25. Bronze, cast, 49 mm., with loop for suspension. This is in the possession of Dr. Thomas Henderson, whom I have to thank for permission to illustrate it here ; I shall refer to it henceforward as the Henderson medal.

The inscription is perfectly straightforward and can only mean ' Messiah-King has come in peace, and Man-God, exalted, made living '.

The point which should be noticed is that, unlike all others of the Hebrew group, this medal employs marks of punctuation after the words for ' peace ' and ' God ', and further that the ends

Fig. 25.—Medal in the possession of Dr. Thomas Henderson.

of two other words are definitely marked by the final *m* which is used in the words for ' man ' and ' exalted ' ; in fact, the inscription is much more careful and literate than any that we shall find in the rest of the group. Now with the exception of the word רם, which Albonesius may have found obscure, this inscription bears the sense that he gives. We may therefore not unreasonably assume that, though our medal may be—as it looks—later than his time, it represents a type similar to that which he saw.

The four letters on the obverse are, I would suggest, to be read with the initial *aleph* as common to both upper and lower lines thus ‏וי‏ ‏ש‏} א, i. e. { Man [1]
                                      { God

---

[1] איש, it is true, is rather *vir* than *homo*, but may have been used (1) in order to obtain a short word, (2) because it contains two of the letters of the name Jesus.

We next come to the Hebrew medals of the kind which has been hitherto associated with the observations of Albonesius. Innumerable specimens exist, made at different times from the sixteenth century to the present ; but the great majority are bad casts of quite recent date. They are to be described as follows :

Fig. 26.—' Hebrew ' medals in the British Museum.

(2) *Obv.*—Bust of Christ l., exactly of the type of the XPS · REX medal, but without the cross ; across the field, square Hebrew inscription [1] א ישׁו

Rev.—Square Hebrew inscription in five lines :

משיח

מלך באבש

לום וארמא

רם עשׁוי

חי

[1] The last letter is frequently made like a *iod* instead of a *waw*.

Fig. 26, *a*, *b*, and *c*. Bronze and various base metals, cast; five specimens in the British Museum measure from 42 to 24 mm.; on one of the smaller the inscription is much blundered. In fig. 26 *c* the bust is rather differently treated, and on both sides there is a narrow wreath border. In the Berlin Cabinet is a small pendant measuring only 21 mm. A badly-blundered specimen which was found in Peru, and of which there is a photograph in the Department of Coins, British Museum, has, incised on the obverse, the words **OS NON COMMINVETIS EX EO** (St. John xix. 36). Cf. M. Schwab in *Rev. Num.*, 1892, p. 253, no. 30; S. Ferarès, *ibid.*, 1917, pp. 269 ff., pl. X, A–F. C. Waser (*De ant. Numis Hebr.*, 1605, fol. 62 verso) describes a silver specimen; and another in the same metal belonged to H. Battandier, *Rev. de l'Art chrétien*, 1899, pp. 418 ff.

This is the commonest of all medals of Christ.

(3) A variety, unique so far as I know, was included in the Murdoch Collection (fig. 27).[1] It is of gold, and much smaller than the usual size. The obverse differs from the others in having a cross at the back of the head of Christ (a feature borrowed from the **XPS · REX** medal); it has also been chased, and is on the whole the most carefully executed specimen of this class of medal that I have seen. The inscription on

Fig. 27.—Medal formerly in the Murdoch Collection.

the reverse is, however, no better than is found on most other specimens of the second variety of the Hebrew medal.

(4) Another variety of this medal, which I have recently seen, is of base metal, of the same size as the last, and has a wreath-border on both sides; the hair is arranged in three long plaits, and the treatment of the features shows some attempt at characterization. Unfortunately it is too badly preserved to repay reproduction.

(5) Another kind (fig. 28) has no letters on the obverse; on the reverse is a different inscription in four lines

ישוע

נצרי משיח

יהוה ואדם

יחד

Fig. 28. Bronze, cast, 34 mm. British Museum. Cf. M. Schwab, *Rev. Num.*, 1892, p. 253, no. 31; S. Ferarès, *ibid.*, p. 278, pl. X, x.

The inscription on this medal means 'Jesus of Nazareth, Messiah, God and Man in one'.[2]

[1] Sotheby's Sale Catalogue of the Murdoch Collection, 1904, lot 983, Pl. xxx.

[2] M. Schwab's rendering, 'Jésus, Nazaréen, oint de Dieu et des hommes ensemble', is quite unacceptable.

It remains to consider the inscription on nos. 2, 3, and 4.[1] About the first four words there is little controversy; they mean 'Messiah-King came in peace'.[2] The last two words also offer no difficulty; there is general agreement that they mean ' has been made living ', i.e. *incarnatus est*.[3] The difficulty is in the middle words, a complex of seven letters. On none of the pieces that I have seen can they be transliterated, as M. Schwab proposes, ו־אומא‎ | ‎ום (for? אומים‎, ' in the midst of the nations '), and this reading may be dismissed. There is much more to be said for the view of Caspar Waser,[4] who read the letters *veor meadam*, translating the whole of the latter part of the inscription *et lux de homine facta est*. This, however, does not give due

Fig. 28.—Medal in the British Museum.

force to the last word חי‎ (' living '). If we accept Waser's transliteration, we should see in the words a reference to the text (St. John i. 4): *et vita erat lux hominum*. I confess that this approximation to a text of the Gospel seems to me very strong evidence in favour of Waser's transliteration. The distinction between ד‎ and ר‎ (*d* and *r*) is difficult in square Hebrew at the best of times; but it is observable that on the specimen which M. Ferarès singles out as the best written,[5] the rounded

---

[1] It also occurs on a medallion of another type (see above, p. 45).

[2] Only Ferarès (*loc. cit.*, p. 272), for some reason, translates the verb by the imperative, ' viens '.

[3] Ferarès maintains that the word עשוי‎ is a Rabbinic or Talmudic, rather than a biblical, form, and builds up on this foundation an elaborate theory which collapses, as we shall see, on examination. Reference to a concordance shows that עשוי‎ is no more exclusively Rabbinic than *factus est* is exclusively mediaeval. Mr. G. Margoliouth considers that the last words, even allowing for the fact that the inscription was composed by some one who knew but little Hebrew, can hardly mean ' was made incarnate ', but rather ' came to life again ', as M. Schwab renders it. But it is surely impossible to insist on such a subtlety.

[4] *De antiquis Numis Hebr.*, 1605, fol. 62 *verso*. But the correct form is אור‎, not אר‎.

[5] F on his plate X.

form of the third letter, as contrasted with the angular form of the sixth letter, in the complex under discussion, is distinctly in favour of Waser's reading וארמאדם. On the other hand, on all the other specimens the doubtful letters seem to be made exactly alike, as ד. We cannot read וארם אדם (*ve-adam adam*) because on all the specimens the fourth letter has the medial or initial, not the final, form of *m*.[1] Therefore, if we do not accept Waser's reading, we must divide the words וארמא רם (or רם). Of these two readings the former alone makes any kind of sense, and the reading רם (*rm*) is supported by the inscription on the Henderson medal. It can only mean ' exalted ' or ' is (*or* was) exalted '.[2] It remains to explain the form ארמא, with the final *aleph* instead of אדמה. This *aleph*, Dr. Barnett suggests, may well be the Aramaic suffix ; to the present day there are to be found pieces of Aramaic side by side with Hebrew in such documents as marriage contracts. But it is also possible that it is a relic of the word אל, as we find it on the Henderson medal. It may be conjectured that the man who first made the model for the piece under discussion had before him an imperfectly preserved specimen of the Henderson type, on which the ל of אל (coming as it does at the edge) was damaged and obscure. He may have known a little Hebrew, not enough to make him supply the missing letter, but enough to make him (when he dropped the final ל of אל, and tacked the א on to the preceding word) alter the final form of *m* in that word to the medial form. If this conjecture be correct, we have in our puzzling inscription only a broken-down version of that on the Henderson medal. But the interpretation of the inscription on Waser's lines, bringing it into relation with the text of St. John mentioned above, still seems to me the most plausible.

The most recent interpretation of the inscription is also the most ingenious, but not for that reason the most acceptable. M. Ferarès believes the legend to be deliberately distorted, in order to convey a hidden meaning by means of puns and allusions. Thus the last word but one, עשׁי (which, as we have seen, he wrongly considers to be a Rabbinic or Talmudic form) can, he says, be read backwards as יׁוׁשע='Ιωσῆς, one of the Hebrew

---

[1] In this differing from the inscription on the Henderson medal.

[2] So Dr. Barnett assures me, in contradiction of Ferarès' rendering, ' raises up '.

names of Jesus. This would suggest the subversion of Christianity. He suspects a play of words in וארמא; if the author had intended to say ' and the earth ', והארמה would have been more correct. The apparent sense of the inscription he takes to be ' Messiah-King, come in peace, and let the earth exalt him who maketh life '. But there is no reason for translating ' come ' instead of ' is come ', and the voices which he adopts for the two other verbs appear to be unjustified. In his translation, such as it is, he finds a *résumé* of a verse of the *Revelation* of St. John (xxii. 17) : ' And the Spirit and the bride say, Come. And he that heareth, let him say, Come. And he that is athirst, let him come : he that will, let him take the water of life freely.' It must be confessed that *résumé* is an odd word to use in this connexion ; most readers will fail to see the slightest relation between the two texts. Even were the connexion established, the use of a reminiscence of a passage from the *Revelation*, rather than from the Old Testament, would hardly support, as M. Ferarès seems to imply that it does, the contention that the author was not a Christian. The use of Rabbinic or liturgic Hebrew which he professes to discover in the last word but one shows, he argues, that the inscription was drawn up by a learned Jew, who further concealed in it an anti-Catholic invocation ! If we point the much-discussed seven letters וְאֶרֹמא רֹם, we get ' and Heathen Rome ', the word Edom designating the Roman Empire, which in the Talmud is a synonym of heathendom ; this use of Edom for Rome was current in the days of the Inquisition, and the censors often suppressed it in Jewish writings. The hidden sense is accordingly revealed as ' Messiah-King, come in peace, and (let) heathen Rome be (re-)made living '; in other words, ' let the Roman Empire be revived' by the subversion of Christianity. That is to say, an orthodox (or forcibly converted) Italian Jew invokes his Messiah who shall bring about the revival of the Roman Empire and thereby the overthrow of the Kingdom of Christ, whose image he wears on the other side of the medal ; and the medal must date from one of the periods when persecution under the Inquisition was at its height. It is assumed that to the Italian Jews the Roman Empire, as the enemy of Christianity, wore a favourable aspect. But is it conceivable that any orthodox Jew should have actually wished for the restoration of Pagan Rome, which to any one who thought of the destruction of Jerusalem must have been anathema, and throughout all Jewish history was a type of brutal and immoral government ?

The puzzling word on the obverse of these medals also affords a field for the ingenuity of M. Ferarès. א has been interpreted as an abbreviation of אדון (*adon*, ' Lord ') ; but, as he says, we might as logically regard it as the abbreviation of the word אנוכי (' I am '). ישו is an incorrect writing of ' Jesus ' ; it should end in ע, as in Rouille's engraving (above, p. 46, fig. 24). He therefore rejects the interpretation of the word as ' Lord Jesus ' or ' I am Jesus ', and reads the letters as date-numerals. Thus א 1, י=10, ש=300, ו=6, making 317. Assuming the omission of the thousands numeral, he makes the equation 5317 (of the Jewish era of 3760 B.C.)=A.D. 1557. But he gives no explanation of the arrangement of the letters in their peculiar order.

If M. Ferarès is right, the Roman Jews played an extremely clever trick on their persecutors, inducing them to accept, and distribute to forcibly converted Jews, a medal which was ostensibly Christian, but which bore a hidden sense, comforting the wearer with the hope of the destruction of the dispensation to which he was compelled to submit. Attractive as such a solution of the puzzle may seem to some minds, most dispassionate critics will regard it as so excessively ingenious as to arouse suspicion. The Henderson medal, and the variety illustrated in fig. 28, show that the type was used with inscriptions bearing a perfectly straightforward sense. We have no right to look for a cryptic meaning in the other inscription if we can explain it on the assumption of clumsiness or illiteracy.

Another speculation of M. Ferarès—there is no limit to his ingenuity—concerns the authorship of the medal. Incidentally, he discovers that, since the word *adam* means ' red ', the last words of the inscription may also convey the sense ' it is made by the celebrated Rossi '. The portrait of Christ on this medal has, as we shall see, actually been attributed to the well-known medallist Giovan Antonio de' Rossi. The Rossi were one of the four families which claimed to have been brought to Rome by Titus as prisoners after the fall of Jerusalem. On numismatic grounds, there is no objection to the attribution, which is due to the late Henri de la Tour.[1] He bases it on the resemblance of the

[1] *Bull. de la Soc. Nat. des Ant. de Fr.*, p. 385. The cast from which the medal by Rossi is illustrated in fig. 29 was kindly sent me by M. de la Tour.

head to that on a medal struck by order of Pius V in his sixth year (1571–2) ; this medal, which is signed by Rossi, I reproduce (fig. 29) from the specimen in the Bibliothèque Nationale :

Bust l. of Jesus Christ, draped, as on the XPS · REX and other medals, but only rays (arranged cross-wise) behind the head. Inscription : EGO SVM LVXMVNDI. Below the bust, IO · ANT · R · M · F ·

Rev.—Adoration of the Magi. Inscription : ILLVMINARE HIERVSALEM ; below, PIVS · V · P · M · ; below the Virgin, AN · VI.

Bibliothèque Nationale (fig. 29). Bronze, struck, 34 mm. Armand, i, p. 244, 4.

Bonanni [1] says of a medal with this same reverse that it was made to celebrate the numerous conversions of Jews which

Fig. 29.—Medal by G. A. de' Rossi, in the Bibliothèque Nationale.

signalized the pontificate of Pius V. M. de la Tour infers from this that the Hebrew medals were cast at the same time and for the same reason ; and may, he thinks, considering the profession of faith on the reverse, have been meant for distribution to new converts.

Bonanni, however, says nothing of a medal with a head of Christ. As he does not describe the obverse of the medal with the Adoration of the Magi, it is to be assumed that it was a bust of the Pope (probably by Federigo Parmense, as on a specimen in the British Museum) and not of Christ. We know that the dies kept in the Papal Mint were frequently combined in various ways ; and there is, therefore, some doubt as to whether Rossi's head of Christ is directly connected with the Adoration of the Magi, and so with the conversion of Jews, in the pontificate of Pius V.

However this may be, there is no doubt that Rossi did put his signature to the somewhat banal type of Christ which we are discussing. The question is : when did he do it ? Was it in 1557, as M. Ferarès would have us believe, on the ground

[1] *Numismata Pontificum*, i, p. 292.

of his interpretation of the four letters accompanying the bust ? Historically, there is no objection to that view.[1] We know that Rossi came to Rome in 1544 ; his signed medals of the Popes Marcellus II and Paul IV are dated 1555 and 1556, but he went to Florence quite at the beginning of 1557, since a document dated January 29 of that year records a payment to him of salary from the duke. This date does not, of course, square exactly with M. de la Tour's theory of the association of the medal with the conversion of Jews in 1571–2. But, as we have seen, the die may have been cut by Rossi for an earlier reverse than that with which alone it is now associated, the present combination being due to the authorities of the Papal Mint in 1571–2. It should be observed that acceptance of M. Ferarès' dating of the medal does not commit us to the rest of his theories. On the other hand, if we reject his dating, and assume that the combination of obverse and reverse in the medal at Paris is authentic, it does not by any means follow that Rossi actually designed the obverse of the Hebrew medal himself. Both obverses, Rossi's and that of the Hebrew medals, go back, perhaps independently, to a type which was certainly popular before 1553 (the date of Rouille's publication, fig. 24), and the finest rendering of which is seen in the XPS · REX medal. Who made that medal, we do not know ; but it has a certain refinement and dignity which make it impossible to attribute it to Rossi himself, whose cast medals are rather coarse and loose in treatment.

What then was the object for which these medals were made ? M. Léon Germain[2] has shown that the formula *Christus rex venit in pace, Deus homo factus est,* came into use towards the end of the fourteenth century, and was especially in vogue in the fifteenth and sixteenth centuries, as an incantation against demons. For that reason it is especially common on bells of the time. There is nothing improbable in the theory, proposed by M. Germain, that these medals were made and used as charms. At any rate, we know that in the seventeenth century they were frequently met with and were commonly to be seen suspended

---

[1] For a sketch of Rossi's career see C. von Fabriczy, *Italian Medals* (trans. by Mrs. Hamilton), p. 189 ; also V. Poggi, ' Di un cammeo di Giovan Antonio de' Rossi ', in *Riv. d' Arte,* ix, 1916.

[2] *Rev. de l' Art chrétien,* 1900, pp. 418 ff. In his most recent contribution to the subject (cited above, p. 47, note 2) he continues to maintain his view of the talismanic object of the medals.

to the necks of children.[1] The motive underlying this custom is explained by the following passage from an eighteenth-century numismatist :

' I was lately asked by an honest fellow what was the meaning of the " penny " which his child had up to that time worn round his neck. His pastor had once seen it, and had said that this superstitious coin should not be any longer hung round the child's neck. His wife thought it was a charm against the falling sickness, and had made all her children wear it hitherto ; but if it was anything evil and magical, he would have it put away. I answered that I had never devoted myself to the explanation of Hebrew coins, and he ought rather to ask the pastor. Then, since the pastor had disapproved of the child's wearing the coin, he would be able to tell him the reason why he held it to be superstitious. A few days afterwards he came to me again, and reported that in reply to further questioning the pastor had said that it was a scandalous abuse of the name and likeness of Jesus Christ to suppose that a " penny ", on which they were found, could defend children from the falling sickness '.[2]

This use of the medal as an amulet is probably now obsolete ; but there is little to choose between the superstition which inspired it and the credulity which makes it worth the while of an enterprising firm (whose name, *ne castissimas eius aures offendam*, I suppress) to issue copies of the medal. The following advertisement accompanies a very bad cast-iron reproduction of the medal, which is, or used to be, easily procured in London, and seems to belong to the same school of art as the reproduction of the false shekel with which I have dealt elsewhere.[3]

With the Compliments of the Manufacturers :

The —— —— Stove Co., Ltd., B'ham.

The First-Century Portrait of Christ.

ONE OF THE EARLIEST LIKENESSES OF OUR LORD.

THIS Medal is a facsimile of a remarkable coin made in the first century of the Christian era, and contains a unique portrait of the Saviour. The original was discovered in the Campo dei Fiori (the Jew Market) in

---

[1] Surenhusius, in his edition of the Mishna, quoted by Albert Way in *Archaeological Journal*, xxix (1872), pp. 115 f.

[2] J. D. Köhler, *Münz-Belustigung*, part vi (1734), pp. 353 f.

[3] See below, pp. 82 f.

Rome. The obverse contains a portrait of Christ, the reverse side an inscription in Hebrew characters, which reads : ' The Saviour has reigned, he came peacefully ; having become the light of man, He lives ' (or lived). It is well known that the first Christians in Rome, owing to the terrible persecutions to which they were submitted, were compelled often to meet in secret. Such a coin, it is believed, was used as a token to admit members to their meetings in the Catacombs, and was carried by early converts as a means of recognition without exchange of words.

The ' original discovered in the Campo dei Fiori ' was a specimen *purchased* there by M. Boyer d'Agen in the spring of 1897, and published with much pomp by its purchaser. His error was exposed by M. Battandier [1] and others,[2] but continues to flourish exceedingly.

The bust of Christ by Rossi, which we have described above, cannot in any sense be regarded as an original creation. It is, as we have hinted, merely a poor modification of the XPS · REX type, from which the Hebrew medal is also descended. The work, which is hard and uninteresting, does not excel, and is often surpassed by, that of numerous other medals produced, especially at the Papal Mint, from about the middle of the fifteenth century onwards.

I describe here a certain number of these later medals. It would, doubtless, be easy to add to them.

(1) Bust of Christ l., as on the XPS · REX medals, but with circular halo at back of head. Around, inscription, IESVS · NAZARENVS · REX · IVDEORVM.

Rev.—Calvary ; in the centre, Christ on the cross, above which are the sun and moon ; to l., the Virgin ; to r., St. John with hands clasped looking up. Around, Hebrew inscription, ' Jesus of Nazareth, King of the Jews '.

British Museum (fig. 30). Bronze gilt, cast, 44 mm.

(2) Bust of Christ l., draped, with long soft hair and beard ; around, inscription, EGO SVM VIA VERITAS ET VITA.[3]

Rev.—Calvary ; in the centre, Christ on the cross between two thieves ; in the background, numerous horsemen ; in the

[1] *Rev. de l'Art chrétien*, 1879, pp. 418 f.
[2] As H. de la Tour, E. Babelon. See S. Ferarès in *Rev. Num.*, 1917, pp. 269 f. I have not seen the brochure (' Notice sur la Médaille du Campo dei Fiori ') in which M. Boyer d'Agen attempted to reply to M. de la Tour ; but the modern origin of the medal does not admit of dispute. The character of the Hebrew script is in itself enough to disprove its antiquity ; nor can any one who has any knowledge of the development of style in coins and medals for a moment think of placing its origin earlier than the sixteenth century.
[3] St. John xiv. 6.

foreground, on the left, the fainting Virgin with the Maries and St. John ; on the right, group casting lots.

Bronze, cast.

Milan, 89 mm. Armand, ii, p. 7, no. 2.

Museo Nazionale, Florence, 88 mm. Supino, p. 191, no. 608.

British Museum, 74 mm. (fig. 31). Keary, nos. 278, 279.

[In our illustration, the obverse is given from Keary, no. 278, the reverse from Keary, no. 279, which is a lead cast of the reverse only.]

Fig. 30.—Medal in the British Museum.

Fig. 31.—Medal in the British Museum attributed to Leone Leoni.

This, after the XPS · REX medal, is undoubtedly the finest of all the sixteenth-century medals of Christ. In the treatment of the profile and hair, and in the drapery, the artist shows an originality which places him considerably above the ordinary level of copyists. The medal has been attributed to Leone Leoni, on grounds of style, and also for the reason that the Crucifixion of the reverse is found associated[1] with a medal of Cardinal Granvelle (of whom he made numerous medals). Leone Leoni (1509–90) was employed at the Papal Mint in Rome from 1537 to 1540; in 1541 he made his well-known medal of Andrea Doria, and from this time until his death in 1590 he was for the most part employed at Milan, although he made numerous journeys to Venice, Parma, Rome, and even out of Italy. Unfortunately,

Fig. 32.—Medal in the British Museum.

the attribution to him of this medal cannot by any means be regarded as certain.

(3) The same type, reduced, appears on a bronze medal found at Castel di Sangro, and published by Lorenzo Fiocca;[2] a cruciform arrangement of rays is added behind the head, and the inscription is ·SALVATOR· ·MVNDI· On the reverse is a bust of a Virgin to r., nimbate and veiled, with the inscription REGINA *CAELI*. The correspondence with the type of the

[1] This argument has very little validity, since obverses are constantly found associated with reverses which were not made for them or by the same hand.

[2] *Rassegna d'Arte*, 1913, p. 119, fig. 8. Diameter, judging from the illustration, 40 mm.

medal attributed to Leone Leoni and the whole character of the work make it impossible to accept Fiocca's attribution to the fifteenth century, much less to an artist working so early in that century as Amico di Bartolommeo.[1]

(4) The same type of head appears on a medallion worn by Pius IV (1559–65) on a bust in the Victoria and Albert Museum ; but as the bust is not contemporary, being a companion to one of Sixtus V (1585–90), this is no evidence of date.

(5) Bust of Christ l., as on the Hebrew medals, but the head surrounded by rays. Around, inscription, EGO SVM VIA VERITAS ET VITA. At beginning and end of inscription, a leaf.

Rev.—None.

British Museum (fig. 32). Bronze gilt, cast, 88 mm. Keary, no. 277. Other specimens are in the Brera (89 mm.) and Florence (85 mm.) cabinets, and in Mr. T. W. Greene's Collection, with a reverse of Calvary ; so also the Lanna specimen (*Catal.*, 355, 89 mm.). Mr. Maurice Rosenheim has one, without reverse, set in a heavy moulded border, making the diameter 106 mm. The type was adapted to a rectangular field on a plaquette in Berlin dated 1695 (*Ital. Bronzen*, no. 1310).

The resemblance of this medal to the preceding is quite superficial ; it is a comparatively poor work, and belongs to the same type as the Hebrew medals. An attribution to Giovan Antonio de' Rossi is not quite out of the question. With it and them should be compared a crystal intaglio in the British Museum (Franks Bequest) with the same legend, but without the rays behind the head (fig. 33).[2]

(6) In the Berlin Cabinet is a reduction (32·5 mm.) of the medal just described, but of rather better style, in spite of the clumsy way in which the lettering passes over the rays of the halo. (fig. 34). On the reverse is a bust of the virgin, with the legend FECIT MIHI MAGNA QVI POTENS EST (St. Luke i. 49). Did specimens of the larger medal exist with a similar reverse ? I doubt it, as the bust of the Virgin is not quite in the same style as the bust of Christ on the obverse.

(7) In the same connexion may be mentioned a large bronze medallion (114 mm.) in the collection of Mr. Henry Oppenheimer. The bust has no halo. Across the field are the words יהוה ישועה (' Jehovah, Jesus '). On the reverse is משיח מלך הלך בשלום ויהוה בעלמה לאיש שתל (שָׁתַל for ?) נעשה אנוש ישועה.

[1] An inscription shows that he was working in 1422, long before the art of the medal was originated by Pisanello.

[2] Dalton, *Catal. of Engraved Gems*, no. 562, Pl. xx. Sir C. H. Read first called my attention to this intaglio.

Rendered word by word, this inscription would appear to mean, 'Messiah-King has gone in peace, and Jehovah in (or by) a virgin to man a scion (?) has been made man Jesus'. The

Fig. 33.—Crystal Intaglio in the British Museum, and Impression.

Fig. 34.—Medal at Berlin.

Fig. 35.—Medal by Cavino in the British Museum.

general sense is clear, that God has been born of a virgin into the race of mankind as the man Jesus. Dr. Barnett, to whom I owe the interpretation, points out that the style of the lettering appears to be German, a suggestion borne out by the treatment of the bust, which is highly finished but entirely mechanical.

The piece is later than the sixteenth century, perhaps as late as the eighteenth.

(8) Bust of Christ r., of a different type from the Hebrew medals. Around, inscription, PORVS CONSILII FILIVS.[1] Signed on the truncation IOANES CAVIN.

Rev.—The Crucifixion ; in the centre, Christ on the cross, with label INRI ; at its foot, the Magdalen ; to the l., the Virgin ; to the r., St. John. Around, inscription, OMNIA SVRSVM TRACTA SVNT.

British Museum (fig. 35). Bronze, 36 mm. *Zeitschr. f. Num.*, viii. *Verhandlungen*, pp. 10 f. ; Armand, iii, p. 79 ; Supino, p. 117, no. 315. The British Museum specimen is an early cast from the struck original.

(9) Bust of Christ l., draped, r. hand raised in blessing. Around, inscription, IESVS · LIBERATOR · ET · SALVATOR. Signed on truncation 1565 · IOAN · CAVINVS · PA.

Rev.—Triple-headed figure of the Trinity seated to front, wearing tiara, r. hand raised in blessing ; to r. and l., heads of cherubim ; below, two angels trumpeting. Inscription, DEVS · TRINVS · ET · VNVS.

The illustration (fig. 36) is from modern pewter impressions from Cavino's original dies, which are preserved in the Bibliothèque Nationale, Paris. Specimens of the medal are in the British Museum (bronze, cast, 34 mm.) and at Parma (Armand, i, p. 182, no. 19 ; iii, p. 79 *b*). On the obverse the letters ET are in monogram.

(10) Bust r. of Christ, nimbate, draped, bearded, with long hair. Inscription, FIGVRA · ESPRESSA (*sic*) · SVBSTANTIAE · PATRIS.

Rev.—The Transfiguration. HIC · EST · FILIVS · MEVS · DILEC· TVS · IPSVM · AVDITE.

Fig. 37. Bibliothèque Nationale (Coll. Valton), 38 mm. Armand, iii, p. 150 *E*. Attributed by Armand to Cavino. I owe the cast from which fig. 37 is made to the late M. Valton's kindness.

Of the last three medals, the two former certainly, the third possibly, were made by Giovanni dal Cavino, of Padua (1500–70). They all bear but slight resemblance to the usual type, and are poor works of little artistic interest.

(11) Bust of Christ, apparently derived from Rossi's medal ; it has the same inscription (EGO SVM LVX MVNDI) and the same cruciform halo behind the head. The date 1581 is placed below the bust. On the reverse is a plain Latin cross. It is attributed by

---

[1] According to Plato (*Symp.* 203 b) *Poros* (the Way) was the son of *Metis* (Counsel).

du Molinet[1] to the school of the Paduan Cavino. Bolzenthal[2] has pointed out that the date precludes an attribution to Giovanni Cavino, who died in 1570, and has suggested that it may be by his son Vincenzo. It seems to me to show no especial resemblance to the style of the Paduan school.[3]

(12) Bust l. of Christ crowned with thorns; on his breast, a medallion with a facing head. Inscription, EGO · SVM · LVX · M · VIA · VERITAS · ET · VITA.

Fig. 36.—Medal by Cavino (modern impressions from old dies).

Fig. 37.—Medal in the Bibliothèque Nationale (Valton Collection).

Rev.—Christ standing, nude but for waistcloth, holding the cross; in foreground, trees; in background, towers of a city. Inscription, SINE · IPSO · FACTVM · EST · NICHIL.

Collection of Mr. Maurice Rosenheim (fig. 38). Cast, 46 mm.
British Museum. Silver gilt, cast, 46 mm.
Coll. Vasset. Armand, ii, p. 7, no. 3.

In this medal we see for the first time the crown of thorns. It may be compared (to its advantage) with the bust on Valentin

---

[1] C. du Molinet, *Le Cabinet de la Bibliothèque de Ste. Geneviève* (1692), p. 118, no. lv on the plate facing p. 112.
[2] *Skizzen zur Kunstgesch. der modernen Medaillen-Arbeit* (1840), p. 100.
[3] The original dies are in the Bibliothèque Nationale, and I have an impression from them before me.

Maler's medal which bears the inscription, EGO SVM VIA VERITAS ET VITA, and is dated on the reverse 1583 (see below).

The regular series of Papal medals with the bust of Christ seems to begin with the Jubilee of 1550. Very common (13) is a nimbate bust with the inscription BEATI · QVI · CVSTODIVNT · VIAS · MEAS.[1]

Fig. 38.—Medal in Mr. Maurice Rosenheim's Collection.

Fig. 39.—Jubilee Medal of 1550 in the British Museum.

Thus we find it combined with obverses of the arms of Cardinal Guido Ascanio Sforza (in the year of the vacancy of the Holy See, 1550), of the Porta Santa in the Jubilees of the same year under Julius III (fig. 39), and of Gregory XIII in 1575, and with ordinary portrait obverses of Julius III, Paul IV, Pius IV, Pius V, and Gregory XIII. Not only is the type the same, but the same die is used for medals of all the Popes mentioned. The Papal Mint had a practice, disconcerting to students of numismatic history, of making hybrid medals by attaching a reverse made for one Pope to obverses belonging to another ; and it carried this practice to the degree of altering old dies, or making entirely new ones, so that, when the medals struck

[1] Prov. viii. 32.

from them are patinated by age or art, they are frequently very difficult to distinguish from the originals. An almost hopeless confusion thus arises. At least five varieties of the medal in question must be condemned as ' modern strikes ', and indeed there is some reason to suppose that the type may really have first been introduced as late as 1575, and that the combinations with earlier obverses may be due to the activity of later mint-masters. As the specimen illustrated shows, the type has no artistic interest except as being derived—at a very long distance— from the XPS · REX medal. I therefore abstain from what would be a tedious classification of the varieties.[1]

Fig. 40.—Restored Medal of Paul IV in the British Museum.

(14) The small bust of Christ, accompanied by the Hebrew inscription א יש״, which we have already met with on the Hebrew medals (fig. 26), also recurs on the reverse of a medal struck in the first year of Pius IV (1559–65).[2] The same type, though not from actually the same die, is found on an undoubtedly old medal of the Jubilee of Gregory XIII (1575).

Another instance of the mystifications abounding in the Papal series is furnished by the following.

(15) A bust (fig. 40), with rays arranged cross-wise behind the head, appears as the reverse to a medal of Paul IV (1555–9), struck from a cracked die, and without any reverse inscription. It has all the appearance of being copied from Rossi's medal of 1571–2. If this is so, the medal is a ' restitution ', i.e. struck after the death of the Pope whom it commemorates. If it were contemporary with Paul IV, which is unlikely, it would show that Rossi did not even invent the slight modification of the type

[1] Many will be found described in the works of Armand and in Supino's Catalogue of the National Collection at Florence ; see also the earlier works of Bonanni (*Numismata Pontificum*, 1690), and the *Trésor de Numismatique, Médailles des Papes* (1839), and the first edition of the present essay.

[2] Armand, iii, p. 261 *BB* ; *Trés. de Num., Méd. des Papes*, pl. xiii. 7.

with which he has been credited.[1] But the whole appearance
of the medal indicates a comparatively modern origin. I illustrate
it as a warning.

(16) Antonio Abondio (1538–96), a pupil of his father, the
sculptor, Alessandro Abondio the Elder, and probably also of

Fig. 41.—Medal by Antonio Abondio (British Museum).

Fig. 42.—Medal in the British Museum.

Leone Leoni, is responsible for an oval medal of Christ. Although
the type differs in no essential particulars from others of the
latter half of the sixteenth century, but reproduces the profile
of the Hebrew medal, the piece is distinguished by the refinement
which is characteristic of this artist, the last of the great Italian
medallists. It exists in three varieties. That reproduced here
(fig. 41), from a specimen in the British Museum, is of silver,
cast and chased and gilt. It is signed AN : AB : below the bust,
and has the name ישוע in the field behind. The head is sur-

---

[1] Unless Ferarès is right in assigning the origin of the type to 1557 (see above,
p. 55).

rounded by a halo of rays with indented edge, and wears the crown of thorns.[1] The second variety [2] resembles the first in all particulars, save that it is without the crown of thorns. On the reverse is a beautiful composition. Christ, his hands tied, wearing a loin-cloth and an ample mantle fastened with a bulla on his breast, stands to front. About his head is a halo of the same shape as on the obverse ; at his feet, the nails, crown of thorns, and hammer. Two winged putti draw the mantle aside so as to show the figure ; they themselves are half concealed behind the column (about which is twined the cord), and the cross. The reed, with two sponges attached, is seen above the head of the putto on the left.

The third variety [3] is similar to the second, save that on the obverse the Hebrew inscription is arranged across the field, as in fig. 24 above.

(17) Another medal, which Dr. Habich publishes as approaching Abondio in style, is reproduced here (fig. 42) from a specimen in the British Museum (bronze, 42 mm.). On the reverse is represented the Fall. The bust of

Fig. 43.—Pendant by Gasparo Mola in the British Museum.

Christ on the obverse shows an attempt at originality of treatment, which, however, has only succeeded in producing a weak and sentimental expression. It has been dated to the seventeenth century, but the type was known by 1580 (see p. 75).[4]

(18) The latest head of Christ by an Italian medallist that I shall mention is by Gaspare Mola. This artist brings us far into the seventeenth century. His workmanship is able, and the delicate, if not very strong, head which he designed offers a pleasing contrast to the aridity of the heads on most of the Papal medals of the time. His work can be seen on several medals of Urban VIII, Innocent X, and Alexander VII. A good specimen is the little oval pendant in the British Museum [5] here illustrated (fig. 43), with the busts of Christ and the Virgin

[1] Another specimen at Berlin (*Italien. Bronzen*, no. 1253 on pl. LXXIV).
[2] Published by Habich in Helbing's *Monatsberichte*, i, p. 404, pl. iii. 4, 5.
[3] E. Fiala, *Ant. Abondio*, pl. VI. 7. A specimen at Berlin (*Ital. Bronzen*, no. 1251 on plate LXXIV) seems, to judge from the illustration, to have no Hebrew inscription at all.
[4] A specimen at Berlin (*Ital. Bronzen*, no. 1311) is ascribed to that period.
[5] Presented by Mr. Max Rosenheim.

(silver-gilt, 29 by 23 mm.). But it cannot be denied that the work of Mola is lacking in real originality, and is only rendered attractive by his skilful technique.

It would be tedious to dwell longer on these works of a decadent art. The fact is that the Italian medallists were unable to improve upon the XPS · REX type, and therefore, with exceptions such as that doubtfully attributed to Leone Leoni, were content to leave the subject alone, or to produce mere mechanical imitations.

In dealing with the medals of the sixteenth century we have so far confined ourselves to pieces of Italian origin. To discuss in detail the treatment of our subject by German artists would take us too far afield ; I must confine myself to mentioning a few remarkable pieces.[1]

First in importance is a medal attributed to the well-known artist Peter Flötner of Nuremberg.[2] It should, perhaps, have been mentioned at an earlier stage in this investigation, for, as we shall see, it shows traces of derivation from Matteo de' Pasti.

Obv.—Bust of Christ r., draped, with small upstanding locks in the middle of the forehead, hair in long curls on the shoulders ; beard fairly short and curly. Above is the holy dove. The field is filled by an inscription : on l., ICH BIN | DAS LEM | LEIN DAS | DER WE | LT SVND | TREGT IO | HANES | AM ; and on r., I · CAPT | NIMANT | KVMPT | ZV DEM | VATER D | AN DVRCH | MICH IO | AM XIIII.[3] Above is *incised* CRISTVS, and at the end of the legend P · F.

This obverse (fig. 44, left) is found with more than one reverse.

(1) Bust of the Pope to left, with a devil clinging to his tiara : inscription, on l., SO BIN | ICH DAS | KINDT | DER VE |

---

[1] I am indebted for much information about this portion of the subject to my friends the late Mr. Max Rosenheim, whose knowledge of German medals was unrivalled, and his brother Mr. Maurice Rosenheim, who maintains so genially the fine tradition of a splendid collection.

[2] Flötner died in 1546. On his medals see Domanig, *Jahrb. d. kunsthist. Sammlungen*, Vienna, xvi (1895) ; K. Lange, *Peter Flötner* (1897) ; E. Merzbacher, *Beiträge zur Kritik der deutschen Kunstmedaillen* (Munich, 1900), pp. 4 ff. ; and, summing up all recent research, G. Habich, *Deutsche Medailleure*, pp. 101 ff.

[3] i.e. ' I am the Lamb that taketh away the sin of the world ' (John i) ; ' No one cometh unto the Father but by me ' (John xiv).

RDERB | NVS | VND | DER SV | NDEN | SAGT | SANT; and on r., PAVLI|
IN DER | Z EPISTEL | AN DIE T | ESSALO | NICH | ER.[1]

Munich Cabinet, lead, 60 mm. Merzbacher, pl. I. 1.

(2) Crucifixion with many figures. In exergue, inscription :

WIE · DI · SLANG · SO · MOSE · ER · HECHT · | SO · MVS · DER · SVN · DES ·
MENSCHEN | ER · HECHT · WERDEN · AVF · DAS · | ALL · DI · AN · IN ·
GLAVBEN · | HAB · DAS · EWIG · LEBE · | · K · O · S.[2]

Berlin (fig. 44, right). Silver, 60 mm.

(3) Bust of Luther. See Merzbacher, p. 7, with note.

Fig. 44.—Medal with obverse signed by Peter Flötner, in the Berlin Museum.

Of these, the third certainly is by another hand, and need
not concern us. The second also is probably not by Flötner ;[3]
but the first, although the whole specimen is an exceedingly rough
cast, seems to be quite homogeneous in style with the obverse.
It is, however, the obverse[4] with which we are concerned.

Although incised, the word CRISTVS and the signature P · F ·
(on which the attribution to Flötner is based) were, according
to Dr. Domanig, not incised after the casting of this specimen, but
existed in the model from which it was cast.

[1] i.e. ' I am the son of perdition and the
man of sin, saith St. Paul in the second
Epistle to the Thessalonians.'

[2] i.e. ' As Moses lifted up the serpent,
even so must the Son of Man be lifted
up : that whosoever believeth in him may
have eternal life ' (John iii. 14).

[3] It is found combined with an un-
signed obverse (dated 1538) representing
the elevation of the brazen serpent.

[4] Merzbacher mentions a specimen of
the obverse alone (with a wreath-border)
which passed from the Felix Collection
into his own. A leaden cast of the head
alone exists, as Dr. Regling informed
me, in the sculpture collection at Berlin
(among the Italian Bronzes, 1307).

Lange has pointed out that the head shows decided Italian influence. He remarks that the medal of Pasti, and certain plaquettes of the school of the Lombardi (e.g. in the Berlin Museum), show almost exactly the same type and may be regarded as models of the head on the medal. That a specimen of the head itself, cut out, was placed amongst the Italian plaquettes in the Berlin Museum is significant of its resemblance to the Italian works of this kind. After a reference to certain large bronze reliefs of Venetian origin with the facing bust of Christ, which come near to the type, he remarks that it was very popular in Germany in the sixteenth century, as is proved by the many

Fig. 45.—Medal of Count Thomas of Rheineck, by F. Hagenauer, in the British Museum.

silver-gilt pendants with the same profile head, in slightly varied form. To this point we shall return.

The next German medal is very different in character, although of almost exactly the same date.

Bust of Count Thomas of Rheineck l., with fur mantle and cap. Inscription giving his titles as sub-dean and dean of the churches of Cologne, Mainz, and Strassburg.

Rev.—Bust of Christ l., in mantle, with pointed beard, long hair, and radiate cross. Around, inscription, ✱ DVS · IESVS · CRIST · REX VENIT IN PACE CONSCENDENS IN CELOS VIVIT (vine-leaf).

British Museum (fig. 45). Lead, 36 mm.

See *Num. Chr.*, 1904, p. 47, pl. v. 3 ; *Jahrb. d. k. preuss. Kunstsammlungen* xxviii (1907), Tafel M. 1.

This medal is attributed by Dr. Julius Cahn to F. Hagenauer, and dated between 1538 and 1546, and the attribution is accepted by Dr. Habich (who likewise attributes it to the master's Cologne period, 1535–46). In the treatment of the hair, and to a slight extent in the profile, the head of Christ betrays the influence of the ' Salvator ' medals, but otherwise it may be classed with the ordinary sixteenth-century Italian types. Thus the cross at the back of the head connects it with the XPS · REX medal, whereas the style of the beard is closer to the poorer work of the Hebrew medals.

The influence of the Hebrew medals is distinctly perceptible in a piece made at least as late as the end of the sixteenth century, and of Viennese origin.

Bust of Christ l., draped. Inscription, SALVATOR MVNDI. The whole in wreath.

Rev.—Arms on two shields : (1) Double-headed eagle, crowned and displayed ; inescutcheon, a cross. (2) Cross. Inscription, MVN + R P + VIENN. The whole in wreath.

British Museum (fig. 46). Gold, enclosed in an open-work enamelled border, with modern loop for suspension. Size (without border), 38 mm.

An anonymous German silversmith (probably of the Joachimsthal school) is responsible for a shop-piece which shows a bust inspired by the Hebrew medals, inscribed XPS : REX · VENIT · IN : PACE · ET : DEVS : HOMO · FACTV(S EST). On the reverse is the Visitation.[1]

Fig. 46.—Medal in the British Museum.

We next come to two medals of the middle of the sixteenth century.

Bust of Christ l., in high relief, with long beard, pendent moustache, hair in long curls on shoulders ; behind the head, lozenge-shaped halo. Inscription, SALVATOR MVNDI CHRISTI MISERER. The whole in wreath.

Rev.—The Agnus Dei r., with cross and banner. Inscription, AGNVS DEI QVI TOLLIT PCTA MVNDI MDXLIX. The whole in wreath.

Mr. Maurice Rosenheim's Collection (fig. 47). Silver-gilt, 34 mm., with ring for suspension. Cast and chased. A variety at Berlin is undated, and shows the lamb's head reverted.

[1] Erbstein Catal., i (1908), no. 554, pl. 16. This collection contained a number of other medals of Christ, unfortunately for the most part unillustrated.

Bust of Christ of similar type, but facing, and holding orb surmounted by cross. Inscription, SALVATOR MVNDI CHRISTI MIS. The whole in wreath.

Fig. 47.—Medal in Mr. Maurice Rosenheim's Collection.

Rev.—The Agnus Dei r., head reverted, with cross and banner. Inscription, AGNVS DEI QVI TOLLIS PCTA MVNDI 1551. The whole in wreath.

Mr. Maurice Rosenheim's Collection (fig. 48). Silver, 25 mm., with ring for suspension. Struck.

Possibly there may be other varieties of the profile type which

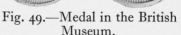

Fig. 48.—Medal in Mr. Maurice Rosenheim's Collection.

Fig. 49.—Medal in the British Museum.

bear out Lange's remarks. But so far as Mr. Rosenheim's larger medal is concerned, the variation from the type represented by Pasti, and even by the Salvator medal of the Berlin Museum, is not slight ; the treatment of profile, hair of the head, beard and moustache, and drapery, is totally different, and I see absolutely no trace of Italian influence, direct or indirect.[1]

On the other hand, so far as regards Italian influence of a general kind, Lange's statement is borne out by a certain number of pieces, such as the variety of the Agnus pendant which I illustrate here (fig. 49). On the obverse we have an Italianizing bust of Christ with the legend EGO SVM VIA VERITAS ET VITA. On

[1] Dr. Regling informed me that among the many other German medals, &c., with heads of Christ in the Coin-cabinet and Collection of Christian Sculpture at Berlin, there is absolutely nothing which has any relationship with the Flötner type of head.

the reverse, the Agnus Dei, with head facing, and the legend ECCE AGNVS DEI QVI TOLLIT PECCATA.

Italian influence is also plainly visible on a certain class of pendants, very different from those represented by Mr. Rosenheim's specimens. The examples [1] next to be described are in the Munich Cabinet.

The first (fig. 50) is a medal of Johann Schmauser, Abbot of Ebersberg (1584–90).[2] The obverse is an unskilful copy of the bust and legend of the XPS · REX medal. The lettering is somewhat blundered ; thus the N's are reversed ; we have LT

Fig. 50.—Medal of Johann Schmauser of Ebersberg, at Munich.

for ET, and IOMO for HOMO ; and the engraver, having miscalculated his space, has not been able to complete the inscription. On the reverse are the arms of the foundation (a boar walking up hill) and of the Abbot (a chalice) with mitre and crozier, and the letters I A (for Iohannes Abbas). The devices on both sides are enclosed in rude wreaths.

A second medal of the same Abbot (fig. 51) copies on the obverse the head of Christ from the medal with the Temptation of Adam (p. 68), placing the letters IHS XPS across the field. But in adopting this type the Abbot was simply following his predecessor Sigismund Kundlinger, who is represented by a piece on the reverse of which are the Abbot's arms, his name SIGISMVNDVS · ABBAS · IN · EBERSPERG, and the date 1580.[3] The same head was used by an Abbot of Attel (probably Engelbert I, 1573–1603) on

[1] Casts of these were supplied by the late Professor Riggauer and his successor in the directorship of the Munich Cabinet, Dr. Habich.

[2] Published by Beierlein in *Ober-*

bayerisches Archiv für vaterländ. Gesch., vol. xxvi (Munich, 1865–6), No. 51, p. 363.

[3] Beierlein, *op. cit.*, vol. xv (1854), pl. 2, no. 43.

a silver medal, on the reverse of which are engraved his arms and the arms of the foundation with mitre and crozier and the initials E · A.[1]

The medallist Valentin Maler (who worked in Nuremberg, Augsburg, and elsewhere from 1563 until after 1596) produced a medal with a neat but quite uninspired head of Christ derived from the Hebrew medals (fig. 52, pewter). The inscription on the obverse (which is signed VM) is DOMIN(VS) REGIT ME ET NIHIL MIHI DEERIT (Ps. xxii. 1). On the reverse is an elaborate allegory of the Church (S. ECLESIA) between the kneeling figures of Poverty (INOPIA) and Gratitude (GRATITVDO), with the legend

Fig. 51.—Medal of Johann Schmauser of Ebersberg, at Munich.

IMPINGVASTI IN OLEO CAPVT MEVM ET CALIX ME(VS) INEBRI(ANS) QVA(M) PRÆC(LARVS) EST (Ps. xxii. 5). On a tablet under the figure of the Church is XPS · LVC · 2 ·, and the whole is signed V.M. C(VM) PRIVI(LEGIO) CÆ(SARIS), indicating the artist's possession of a patent from the Emperor.

Similar in composition, though better conceived and modelled, is the head of Christ on a medal made by Valentin Maler for Ulrich, Abbot of Zweth, in 1597.[2] But Maler's best treatment of the subject is on a piece executed in 1583 (fig. 53). The bust of Christ, which is crowned with thorns, is not merely accomplished but dignified ; the inscription is EGO SVM VIA VERITAS ET VITA. The artist's initials VM are incised on the truncation of the bust, and he has added the words C(VM) PRI(VILEGIO) CÆ(SARIS). On the reverse is a nude Christ, with the cross resting on his shoulders ; the inscription (from Isaiah) is ET LIVORE EIVS SANATI SVMVS ESA. 53, and the note C · PRI · C · is repeated with the date 1583.[3]

[1] Ibid., no. 44.

[2] E. Fiala, Antonio Abondio (Prag. 1909), p. 50, no. 96, pl. x. 10. Habich in Archiv für Medaillen- und Plaketten-kunde, i, p. 107.

[3] Specimens in the Erbstein Catalogue, i (1908), no. 558, pl. 11 (48 mm.), and in the Victoria and Albert Museum.

This must suffice as an indication of the treatment of the subject by German medallists. It could only be exhausted by some one enjoying access to German collections. What we have seen, however, and what we know of German medallic work of the later sixteenth century, make it fairly certain that search in those quarters would not reveal anything original in treatment or conception.

Fig. 52.—Medal by Valentin Maler, in the British Museum.

Fig. 53.—Medal by Valentin Maler, in the Victoria and Albert Museum.

The study of the medals of Christ has introduced us to one or two works of art of good quality, and a great crowd of mediocrities, for which the description 'shoddy' is hardly too strong. It confirms the experience which may be gathered from other fields, that the influence of the devotional spirit, after the primitive stages of artistic development have been passed, is, if not precisely inimical, at least not actively favourable to good art. Religious medals, considered as a whole, may be placed on the same artistic level as hymns. But like hymns, apart from their devotional aspect, they have a certain interest which makes them a fitting, if modest, subject for investigation.

II

FALSE SHEKELS

THE medals of Christ with a Hebrew inscription, described in the preceding essay, are admirable instances of the eagerness with which the pious-minded will accept as ancient anything which pretends to be a monument of Biblical history. The forgeries with which we are now to deal owe their unfailing popularity to the same tendency. They cannot have been a profitable fraud ; but every numismatist knows that the forger by no means always works for a material gain. The passage quoted at the end of this essay shows that his intentions may be highly moral, even when he is not merely displaying his art for the fun of the thing.

In order to appreciate the fraud, it is necessary first to acquaint ourselves with the genuine Jewish shekel. We need not here enter on the vexed question of the exact date of the famous series of Jewish shekels and half-shekels, bearing the dates of five consecutive years. Suffice it to say that while they have long been traditionally attributed to the time of the revolt of Simon Maccabaeus, the theory which is now most generally accepted ascribes them to the time of the first revolt against Rome, which lasted from spring, A.D. 66–7, to autumn, A.D. 70–1.[1]

The types of all these coins are the same (fig. 54) : on the obverse, a cup with (on all but the coins of the first year) a pearled border round the rim ; on the reverse, a flowering lily. The coins of the first year have a cup with a plain rim. The obverse of the shekels is inscribed in ancient Hebrew characters *Shekel Israel* (' Shekel of Israel ') ; while above the cup is a date expressed by one of the first five letters of the alphabet, accompanied (after the first year) by the initial of the word *shenath* (' year '). The inscription of the reverse of the shekel is *Yeru-*

[1] A full account of the coins is given in the British Museum Catalogue of Greek Coins, *Palestine* (1914). The Maccabaean date has still a number of supporters, but they are faced by the fact, which has recently come to light, that a specimen of the coinage has been discovered in a deposit of the time of the First Revolt. See *Revue Biblique*, April 1914, pp. 234 ff.

shalayim ha-kedoshah (' Jerusalem the Holy ') in all years but the first, which has the ' defective ' form, *Yerushalem kedoshah.*

The half-shekels resemble the shekels, except for the obverse inscription, which is merely *hatsi ha-shekel* (' half-shekel ').

Fig. 54.—Genuine Jewish Shekels and Half-shekels. (British Museum.)

The weights of these coins are : of the shekel, about 220 grains troy ; of the half-shekel, about 110 grains troy. That is to say, they belong to the standard in use in the cities of Phoenicia, such as Tyre and Sidon, and generally known as the ' Phoenician '. What should especially be noticed in the coins is the form of the letters, which are clearly distinct from modern square Hebrew, and the peculiar, thick, dumpy fabric. It is not uncommon for Jews, when their knowledge of the language is only sufficient to be dangerous, to deny the Jewish origin of the coins because the letters are strange to them.

The Second Revolt against Rome (A.D. 132–5) also produced a certain number of shekels.[1] The Jews took the current coins of the country—imperial Roman denarii and drachms and four-drachm pieces of the local provincial mints such as Antioch—and re-struck them with their own types. Out of the four-drachm pieces they made shekels with the representation of a building with fluted columns and a podium, perhaps meant for the Temple which Simeon intended to restore.[2] Attached to this as

Fig. 55.—Shekel of the Second Revolt.

reverse type are a *lulab* and *ethrog* (i.e. the bundle of twigs, &c., and the citron which were carried at the feast of Booths). On the obverse is the name Simeon, on the reverse *Lech-eruth Yerushalem* ('the deliver-ance of Jerusalem') (fig. 55).

The Simeon of these coins is either the false Messiah, Simon Bar Cochba ('son of the star'), the chief leader of the revolt against Rome, or, more probably, Simeon III son of Gamaliel II, president of the Sanhedrin, who died about A.D. 163.[3]

This shekel (which occurs in various slightly modified forms) has not been imitated like the earlier one, and therefore need detain us no longer.

The imitations of the earlier shekel fall into two classes, according as they are intended to deceive the more or less experi-enced collector or the general public. Some of the former merely

[1] A detailed account of the two classes of shekel will be found in the British Museum Catalogue cited above.

[2] This is Professor A. R. S. Kennedy's suggestion ; he points out that the Jews of the third century conceived the Temple more or less in this style (see *Encycl. Bibl.* iv. 4394). He points out, in rejec-tion of the theory of Rev. Edgar Rogers (which recognizes in the type the four pillars for the veil of the Holy of Holies, with a conventional rendering within of the Ark and Mercy Seat) that the details suggest a building of stone. The type

until recently was usually described as the Golden Gate of the Temple.

[3] Professor Kennedy interprets Nasi (the title borne by Simeon on many of the coins) as meaning president of the Council at Jamnia, and adds ' had the Simeon of the Second Revolt been the head of the Rabbinic College there, his name would have been preserved in Jewish tradition along with that of his supporter, Rabbi Aqiba. Simeon was probably a secular leader who had the title Nasi, Ezekiel's favourite term for the Messianic Ruler of the new age '.

take the shape of casts (the originals, of course being struck from dies). Others are actually struck from forged dies, and of these a good example is the piece made by one of the most notorious forgers of ancient coins, Carl Wilhelm Becker (1771–1830). Becker probably achieved his most brilliant results with Roman coins, and, but for the fact that his dies were preserved, some of his productions in this line might pass for genuine among the most experienced numismatists. But most museums possess and use for comparison a series of impressions made from his dies, and from such an impression I reproduce a Jewish shekel of the second year (fig. 56). It is by no means one of his best works. The clumsiness of the lily, the misunderstood foot of the cup, the mean rendering of the letters, and the whole style of the coin make it impossible to mistake it for an antique. Forgers of the present day can do better than this.

Fig. 56.—Becker's forgery of the Jewish shekel.

The imitation of the shekel which forms the subject of *One of the Thirty*, an absurd book written by Hargrave Jennings and published in 1873, is made from a shekel of the first year, with clumsy rendering of lettering and type (only the side with the chalice is figured). The coin is represented as about $1\frac{1}{8}$ inch in diameter, and described (p. 348) as being of the size of a crown piece :

'an old-old-OLD Coin of the size of a crown-piece ; dusk—nay, dark. Dark, even black, as with the occult clouds of the wonders of eighteen centuries—yet hiding deep-down in its centre the intolerable possible spark of an immortal magic fire.'

The figure which Jennings gives in illustration of his effusion is only one of the most recent of a long series of clumsy representations of what may have been a true shekel. Any one who takes the trouble to wade through the interminable literature [1] with which the Biblical antiquaries and critics have encumbered this

[1] The worst engraving of this piece is also the earliest known to me : a piece of the second year, in G. Postel, *Linguarum duodecim Alphabetum* (Paris, 1538). It is reproduced below, fig. 61. Most of the writers in the twenty-eighth volume of Ugolinus's *Thesaurus Antiqui-* *tatum Hebraicarum* (Venice, 1765) deal with the subject. The only writer in the volume who shows much critical sense is Herman Conring, in his *Paradoxa de Nummis Hebraeorum*. Hargrave Jennings's illustration, to judge from the quotation on the page following his title, was probably

subject will find plenty of representations of the same kind, often side by side with the obvious forgery with which we shall now deal.

Every numismatist is familiar with the pieces, generally roughly cast in more or less poor silver, which are passed off as genuine Jewish shekels (fig. 57). The inscriptions are the same as those which we find on the genuine coins, except that they are in modern square Hebrew, and that no date is given. The types approximate to those of the true coin; but instead of the lily with three flowers we have a branch with many leaves; and the chalice is replaced by an object apparently meant, to judge by the fumes arising from it, for a pot full of incense.[1] No one who

Fig. 57.—The ' Censer Shekel ' (British Museum).

has seen the genuine struck shekel could for a moment be deceived by this cast piece. Nevertheless, so few people take the trouble to test the truth of what is told them about Biblical antiquities that tradesmen still find it worth their while to offer for sale facsimiles of these impostures. Before me is an atrociously bad cast facsimile which is or was until recently sold by one of the largest firms of general dealers in all London, together with the following printed description :

CAST-IRON MODEL OF JEWISH SHEKEL

This is a facsimile of a genuine Shekel (called in the Bible ' a piece of silver '), coined by Simon Maccabaeus, who was King of the Jews, B.C. 172–142.

It was issued in the year B.C. 170. It is, therefore, now 2,068 years old.

For thirty ' pieces of silver ' Judas betrayed our Lord. The Hebrew inscriptions on the obverse and reverse mean ' Shekel of Israel ' and ' Liberator of Jerusalem ', and the designs represent the pot of manna and Aaron's rod that budded.

[1] Accordingly I call these forgeries made from Bened. Arias Montanus (1527–98), whose *Ephron, sive de Siclo* is reproduced in Pearson's *Critici Sacri*, vol. viii, 1660, p. 657. censer-pieces, although so far as I know a vessel like this, chalice-shaped and without cover or chains, was not used for burning incense in any ritual, Jewish or Christian.

Quite apart from the initial error of supposing the original of this facsimile to be a genuine Jewish shekel, this short paragraph is well worth study for the other misrepresentations compressed into it. The date of Simon's election to the leadership of the Jews is generally supposed to be 143–142 B.C. Unless, therefore, the worthy person who compiled the paper has other information, I am inclined to think that he has been misled by some comparative table of eras, in which the Seleucid year 170 corresponds to the year 143–142 B.C. It would be interesting to know how he ascertains the exact year in which the coin was issued, since it bears no regnal date. The translation ' Liberator of Jerusalem ' is also new, and may have been suggested by the legend ' Deliverance of Jerusalem ' found on some other coins. At the end of all this it would have been surprising indeed to miss the identification of the types as the pot of manna and Aaron's rod that budded.[1] The implication that the ' thirty pieces of silver' were of this kind was also inevitable; but the history of this matter requires an essay to itself.

Writing in 1859 [2] the late Sir John Evans called attention to an ill-fabricated copy of the spurious shekel, which was on sale in London, and described as ' a correct copy and representation of the old Hebrew money . . . current during the lifetime of our Saviour, for thirty pieces of which He was betrayed by Judas Iscariot '. This was evidently a predecessor of the piece just mentioned.

M. A. Levy,[3] again, a few years later, says that the commonest of the forgeries of the Jewish shekel is a piece exactly corresponding to the one we have described. He mentions other forgeries, but we may for the present confine ourselves to this, the most important—that is, the one which has made most victims. Let us trace its history backwards. We find it in Erasmus Frölich's work on the Syrian kings, published in 1754,[4] among the ' modern Hebrew coins ', which he gives as a warning to collectors. He says that he has seen many specimens, varying in metal, weight, &c., but all manifestly false and modern. He

[1] This is the traditional but unfounded explanation of the types of the true shekel.

[2] *Numismatic Chronicle*, vol. xx, p. 8, note 2.

[3] *Jüdische Münzen* (1862), p. 163. The section of Levy's work relating to forgeries of Jewish coins is translated at length by Madden, *Coins of the Jews* (1881), pp. 314 f.

[4] *Annales Regum et Rerum Syriae* (Vienna, 1754), pl XIX (no. v), and *Prolegomena*, p. 92.

supposes that they are due to an unsuccessful attempt to imitate the true shekels. In J. Leusden's *Philologus Hebraeo-mixtus*[1] it is also illustrated, this time as a genuine shekel ; the types are explained as an incense-cup and Aaron's rod ; and the branch is represented as if it were growing up out of a mound.

In 1671, a specimen was included in a parcel of coins which was deposited in the ball of the spire of St. Nicholas Church in Berlin.[2]

Brian Walton, Bishop of Chester, also occupied himself with shekels,[3] and has illustrated two specimens of our piece, one of silver, the other of bronze : illustrations which he borrowed from J. Morin.[4]

Fig. 58.—Waser's Half-shekel.

Fig. 59.—Waser's One-third-shekel.

The work of Caspar Waser[5] on ancient Hebrew coins was known to Leusden. It is surprising, there-fore, that the genuine shekel, which is tolerably well represented by Waser (pp. 59 f.), should be ignored by the later author. Waser does not represent the false shekel with the censer, but it is worth while to glance at his method of dealing with Hebrew coins. On p. 77 and elsewhere he illustrates what (read-ing hastily) one would take to be a half-shekel of the second year (fig. 58), a one-third-shekel of the third year (fig. 59), and a quarter-shekel of the fourth year. The peculiarity about these illustrations is that while the types and legends are as well represented as in the case of the whole shekel, the letter *shin* (initial of *shenath*, year) is omitted before the numeral. Now, the only genuine shekels and half-shekels on which this initial is absent are those of the first year. Waser betrays himself when he comes to the one-third-shekel (p. 78). Of the exis-tence of this as a coin we have no evidence ; but Waser says : ' It is probable that the types and symbols of this coin were

---

[1] 4th ed., 1739, p. 207.
[2] *Zeitschrift für Numismatik*, vi, p. 139.
[3] *Introductio ad lectionem Linguarum Orientalium* (London, 1655), pp. 30 ff.
[4] *Exercitationes Ecclesiasticae in utrum-*que Samaritanorum Pentateuchum (Paris, 1631), pp. 208–9.
[5] *De antiquis numis Hebraeorum*, &c., Zurich, 1605.

the same as those of the whole shekel, so I figure it here with
the same types, but with this different inscription on the
reverse : *shelishith hasshekel Israel*, third of the shekel of Israel.'
He does not commit himself to any statement that the coin
exists ; but ' it pleases him ' to represent it—' quare libet etiam
eisdem (notis et symbolis) eum figuratum hic exhibere '.   In
the same spirit he has invented and figured the half-shekel
and quarter-shekel ; for, although half-shekels exist, there is no
doubt, from his mistake in the representation of the date, that
he had never seen a real one.[1] Indeed, he admits (p. 71) that
all the many shekels he had ever seen had the letter *aleph* over the

Fig. 60.—From Villalpandus.

cup, i.e. were of the first year ; and it is a curious fact that by far
the greater number of the illustrations in works of this time
represent the shekel of this year.   It seems that Waser, like Arias
Montanus before him, regarded the *aleph* as the indication of the
unit (one shekel), and therefore systematically marked his half-
shekel with a *beth*, his third with a *gimel*, and his quarter with
a *daleth*.[2]

To return to the track of the false shekel.   Villalpandus,[3]
a year before Waser, published a plate representing a number
of Jewish coins, including shekels of which we have no reason
to doubt the authenticity, and also one of the censer-pieces
(fig. 60).   He insists that all these pieces, without exception, are
struck : ' which is so certain and clear upon examination, that
should any one attempt to deny it, he would prove beyond all

[1] The nature of Waser's method was
recognized by J. Morin (*op. cit.*, p. 207).
' Waser's parts of the shekel seem not to
be genuine, but invented to represent
the fractions of which mention is made
in the sacred Scriptures.'

[2] J. B. Villalpandus, *Apparatus Urbis*
ac Templi Hierosolymitani, tome iii,
parts 1 and 2 (Rome, 1604), p. 390,
recognized the inadequacy of Montanus's
explanation, but proposed a worse one
himself.

[3] *Op. cit.*, plate facing p. 378 ; see also
p. 390.

dispute that he was so lacking in knowledge of coins as to be unable to distinguish or separate struck coins from such as are cast or made by any other means.' In the face of such condemnation, one hesitates to assert that Villalpandus was mistaken in regard to the censer-piece ; but his experience, so far as I can discover, is unique. He admits that some doubt has been thrown on the piece ; but while he allows that it is somewhat later than the others which he illustrates, bearing letters of an older form, he still maintains that it is ancient.

This is the earliest numismatic publication of this mysterious piece that I have been able to find ; but there is clear evidence that something of the kind existed at a fairly early date in the sixteenth century. Writing on March 21, 1552, to George III, Prince of Anhalt, Philip Melanchthon says : [1]

'I now send you a silver shekel of the true weight of the shekel, to wit, a tetradrachm, with the inscription as it is depicted in the book of Postellus. I also add some verses, interpreting the rod of Aaron and the pot of incense. . . .

DE VETERI NOMISMATE GENTIS IUDAICAE.

Iusta sacerdotum demonstrat munera Siclus
 Cuius in *Ebraeis* urbibus usus erat.
Ut sint doctrinae custodes, virga *Aharonis*,
 Utque regant mores cum pietate, monet.
Significantque preces calicis fragrantia thura,[2]
 Praecipuum munus sunt pia vota Deo,' &c.

The poem also appears in the collected poems of Melanchthon [3] in a considerably modified form ; lines 5 and 6, for instance, read :

Parte calix alia est impletus thure Sabaeo,
 Hic offerre preces, ut nova thura, iubet.

The verses are quoted by Waser to show that Melanchthon considered the chalice on the shekel (the true shekel, as he thinks) to be not the pot of manna, but a censer. Waser is justified in thinking this, since in the book of Postel, to which we have referred above, the piece is undoubtedly a true shekel or a close imitation (fig. 61). But neither Postel nor Waser seems to have known of the forgery with the censer. Melanchthon, admirable scholar as he was, lived before the days of scientific numismatics ; and if he had one of the censer-pieces before him, we shall not be unjust

[1] Bretschneider, *Corpus Reformatorum*, vol. vii, p. 964.
[2] See below, p. 87, on this symbol of prayer.
[3] *Op. cit.*, vol. x, p. 607.

in supposing that he would identify it with the shekel as represented by Postel. Otherwise it is difficult to understand how he could imagine that a censer was represented.

Melanchthon's letter is thus evidence that the censer-shekel existed as early as 1552.

Another witness, professing to date from a still earlier period, is unfortunately not unimpeachable. In the Uffizi at Florence is a painting[1] attributed to Lucas van Leyden, representing Christ with the instruments of the Passion. In this, the thirty pieces of silver are very clearly represented as thirty of our censer-shekels. Though older authorities, such as Evrard,[2] may have accepted the picture as genuine, later critics have been less generous ; and it seems to be impossible to rely on it as evidence for the existence of the censer-pieces in the time of Lucas (who died about 1530).

Fig. 61.—
From Postel.

It is just possible that the smoking censer of these shekels may have suggested the similar vessel which, as a symbol of prayer ('oratio') is seen on the reverse of a little medal of the Emperor Ferdinand I (1556–64).[3]

Finally, another piece of faulty evidence may be cleared away. It has been said [4] that these shekels were made by Georg Emerich, burgomaster of Görlitz, who, after a pilgrimage to Jerusalem, erected in his native place a reproduction of the Holy Sepulchre and gave these shekels as souvenirs to those who came to see it. This would be interesting, if it were founded on fact ; for Emerich (1422–1507) visited Jerusalem as early as 1465. Thus we should be able to trace the shekels back to the latter part of the fifteenth century. Unfortunately, the only foundation for the statement seems to be the fact that such shekels have for some time past been sold at the Görlitz Holy Sepulchre.[5]

[1] To which my attention was called by Dr. Julius Cahn. The portion of the picture which concerns the present question is reproduced in the *Reliquary* (1904), p. 135.

[2] *Lucas de Leyde et Albert Dürer* (1884), p. 660.

[3] K. Regling, *Sammlung Lanna*, iii, no. 678, pl. 36.

[4] Dannenberg, in *Berliner Münzblätter*, xxiv (April 1903), p. 261.

[5] Professor R. Jecht, the leading authority on Emerich's biography, kindly informed me that there is no documentary evidence of the date when these shekels were first sold there ; on no account does he believe that the practice was instituted by Georg Emerich.

I have hitherto not mentioned a more elaborate variety of this forgery. Our illustration (fig. 62) is reproduced from a specimen in the Paris Cabinet ; and engraving of a similar piece serves as the frontispiece of a pompous little work issued in 1810 by S. Lyon.[1] Lyon's piece was found among ruins near Huntingdon in 1809. The legends on this and similar pieces mean : ' The Lord is the Keeper of Israel, the mighty King (or the King of Glory) in Jerusalem ' and ' The Shekel of David which remained hidden in the Treasury of Zion in the Temple '.[2] The symbols added to the types are mitre, anointing horn, urn, and crown, together with various letters of which the significance

Fig. 62.—Variety of the Censer Shekel in the Bibliothèque Nationale.

is obscure. The vase on the one side is described by Levy as containing a three-fold bough ; and this is also the case with the specimen illustrated by Hottinger,[3] but in the specimens figured here and by Lyon that description hardly applies. Whatever the objects in the vase may be, I am inclined to think that the design is in origin a modification of the censer of the other false shekels.

Some one endowed with more patience than the writer may possibly be able to discover the actual origin of these curious pieces and the object for which they were made. As far as our present lights enable us to decide, it would seem that they were invented not exactly in bad faith, merely to delude the pious

[1] *Explanation of and Observations on an Antique Medal . . . now in the possession of S. Lyon*, London, 1810. There are two specimens of this forgery at Paris ; see *Revue Numismatique*, 1892, p. 244, no. 7. I owe the cast from which fig. 62 is made to the late M. J. de Foville.
[2] See Levy, in Madden, *op. cit.*, p. 316.
[3] *Dissertatio de variis Orientalium Inscr.*, col. 876, pl. v, in Ugolinus, tom. 28.

mind, but rather in that spirit of which we have found traces in the work of Waser, and which was exceedingly prevalent among early antiquaries : the spirit which led them to invent coins of all famous characters, from Adam and Eve onwards ; in a word, the passion for completeness. Perhaps the most naïve expression of this state of mind is to be found in the preface of Guillaume Rouille to his *Promptuaire des Médailles*, one of the earliest systematic works on numismatics.[1]

' In order that no one may, under the Cornelian Law, accuse us of falsification, as though we were issuing false coins, in that we have ventured publicly to display before all eyes fictitious and imaginary figures for good and true ones : may a kind and gracious respect be accorded unto this our free confession ; for no man is bound to perform the impossible. Of the first men, before the deluge and the invention of the art of sculpture and painting, as of Adam, Abraham, and other Patriarchs, we do not deny that the images have been made by us ; but with just and true cause ; for, possessing no first exemplar, we have, out of most true and holy Scripture, and out of grave and veracious authors, with consideration of their nature, their customs, their age, time, place, and deeds, and comparison of all together, made these images so like to the truth, that with reason we should rather be commended than in any wise reprehended. And, moreover, why should less be allowed and less conceded to us than to that most noble sculptor Phidias, who, by studying of a few verses of Homer, conjectured the form of Jove, invisible in its substance, and fashioned the Olympian Jove ? Maybe that Homer is of more credibility than the holy Scripture dictated by the spirit and power of God ? Why should we enjoy less licence than Zeuxis the painter, who, out of the faces and forms of the five Agrigentine virgins,[2] selected by his art, made the figure of the fair goddess ? Why may we do less than Asinius Pollio, who made the images of the authors of the books in his library, out of their writings, before any other Roman ?[3] Why is less

---

[1] *Promptuaire des médailles des plus renommées personnes qui ont esté depuis le commencement du monde*. The passage is quoted by E. Babelon, *Traité des Monnaies grecques et romaines*, vol. i (Paris, 1901), p. 98. I translate from the Italian edition (Lyon, 1553), which is, in some ways, quainter than the French of the same year. There are also Latin and Spanish versions.

[2] The French edition has *cent pucelles* ! The ' fair goddess' should be Helen.

[3] In this passage the writer has misunderstood Isidore (*Orig.* vi. 5), who

allowed to us than to him who, by considering the art of Homer, dead so many ages before, did out of his poems and his spirit conjecture and express his face ? For these reasons we are confident that no blame or fault should be imputed to us for having done such a work. Further, Pliny writes in this wise : " The things which are not, are counterfeited ; and the faces which are not seen beget a desire to see them ; nor is there any greater instance and proof of good fortune in a man than this, that all men should always desire to know who he was." Thus far Pliny. We, therefore, imitating these great examples, without any first model, and following only the truth of history and right reason, have formed and found out, with the counsel and assistance of the most learned of our friends, the images and faces of the first men, and of some of the intermediate ages, to this end only, that our history, being depicted with the pencil as well as with the pen, may not be deficient in the one or the other part.'

merely says that Asinius placed portraits of Greek and Latin authors in his public library ; while Pliny (*Nat. Hist.* xxxv. ii) says that Varro inserted portraits in his volumes ; but neither Asinius nor Varro need be credited with the inventive faculty attributed to them by our author.

Note.—Casts of the censer-shekel (p. 82) were used by the bell-founder John Palmer of Gloucester to decorate various bells cast by him from 1650 to 1663. See H. B. Walters in *Trans. Bristol and Gloucester Archaeol. Soc.*, xxxiv, p. 119.

III

THE THIRTY PIECES OF SILVER

THAT the incident of the Betrayal of Christ for Thirty Pieces of Silver should have had an attraction for the mediaeval maker of legends, and that pieces professing to be the original coins received by Judas should have been treasured as relics, are hardly matters for surprise. There is no lack of literature on the legend which was woven round the story of the Thirty Pieces, and of late years two or three writers have devoted some attention to the supposed relics of the Betrayal. A comparison and analysis of the various forms of the legend have, however, not been instituted, so far as I have been able to discover. As to the relics, the material for study is only to be found in foreign periodicals and works not generally accessible. It seems worth while, therefore, to make some attempt to trace the development of the legend, and to collect the descriptions of the coins which were or are preserved in various sanctuaries.

The earliest extant work in which I have been able to find the legend in a fully developed form is the *Pantheon* of Godfrey of Viterbo, who died in 1191. He gives it in one of his Latin poems in rhyming three-line stanzas,[1] beginning :

> Denariis triginta Deum vendit Galilaeus,
> quos et apostolicus describit Bartholomaeus,
> unde prius veniant, quis fabricavit eos.

Freely translated, and somewhat abridged, Godfrey's account is as follows :[2] ' Ninus, King of the Assyrians, had these coins made, and it was Terah who fashioned them out of gold ; with them the Ninivite king set up his market. The face of the King

---

[1] I follow the text as given by E. du Méril, *Poésies populaires latines du Moyen-Âge*, 1847, p. 321. I may here record my thanks to Miss L Eckenstein and Mr. J. A. Herbert for several refer- ences to literature and documents bearing on the subject of this legend.

[2] If my version is prosy, confused, and disjointed, I think I am justified in saying that the original is hardly less so.

was stamped on these denarii to furnish an example to all time, and to perpetuate his own likeness. The son of this Terah, called Abram, afterwards took away these coins with his wife Sara when, at God's bidding, he went into Canaan. With these coins he bought land from the men of Jericho ; with these also Joseph was bought by the Ishmaelites ; these did wealthy Pharaoh keep in his treasury. These also the mighty Sibyl, the Queen Nicaula, possessed ; even the Queen of the South, who afterwards from the Court of Solomon gave them, a reverent offering, to the Temple. But Nebuchadnezzar, when he spoiled the Temple, carried them away to Babylon, where they were given as pay for soldiers to the kings in Saba. When the three Magi together brought their three gifts, the scripture of the ancients records that the kings whom the strange star called forth brought these coins to God. But when, taught by angelic warnings, these kings had gone home, a most worthy garment was sent down from heaven for the Child ; without seam was it, and of wondrous hue. His Father sent it from heaven ; no woman span it ; it became longer as the Child grew in stature. Now when Herod commanded that the Child should be sought out to be slain, His Mother in fear of death fled to the land of the Nile and lay hidden there. Then these three gifts were left in that hiding-place, the gold, frankincense and myrrh, and the blessed garment of God. Some shepherds came and carried away the gifts. But there was a certain astrologer who removed the gifts which had been left behind. He knew by the stars all the portents of Christ's coming ; he was an Armenian, just and honourable. Now in the time when Christ was teaching, an angel said to this man : Render up the gifts of God which thou hast taken ; let the sacred gifts of God be restored to Him. So the short tunic of the Child was given back, and as Jesus put it on it became of full size. The man saw it, and his mind was troubled and astonished. The thirty denarii which they had brought to God they gave, at the behest of Jesus, to the treasury of the Temple, which denarii they say Judas afterwards received as his price. After the death of Christ Judas brought them back and cast them down in repentance, and hanged himself and burst asunder. Then they gave fifteen denarii for the Potter's Field, and as many to the soldiers who guarded the tomb by night. Perchance thou thinkest, reader, that my words agree not together, since I have written that those coins were of gold ; for the Book speaks of silver. Mark said that the Lord was bought for silver; of coins or of a talent of gold he spoke not. But it is even as I have said; for it was the custom of the ancients to use more than one name for gold, and to call different metals by the name of silver. Know that Saint Bartholomew wrote thus of this matter; his Hebrew discourse to the Armenians tells how the very God was sold for gold :

> Ergo, patente nota, solus negat hoc idiota,
> cuius habent vota non discere facta remota ;
> lectores dociles pagina nostra vocat.'

The ' discourse of St. Bartholomew to the Armenians written in Hebrew ' seems to have disappeared without leaving any other trace ; at least it is ignored by the chief modern authorities on the apocryphal literature. The Coptic Gospel according to St. Bartholomew, or ' Book of the Resurrection of Jesus Christ by Bartholomew the Apostle ', is a Gnostic production, in which Judas plays a considerable part; but the legend of the thirty pieces is not to be found in such portions of it as have been preserved.[1] It may have been to this Gnostic Gospel that St. Jerome referred when he wrote, in the Preface to his Commentary on St. Matthew,[2] that a spurious gospel of St. Bartholomew was in circulation. We may perhaps assume that Godfrey drew from a Latin translation of some legend of Armenian origin. This is suggested by the facts that the *Sermo*, although written in Hebrew, is addressed to the Armenians, and that the hero of the story is an Armenian. The Armenian sources for the story of St. Bartholomew, so far as published, throw no light on the matter.[3]

Very little later than Godfrey of Viterbo is the author of the Syriac *Book of the Bee*,[4] Solomon, who became Bishop of Baṣra about A.D. 1222. In him we find the legend in an elaborate and in many ways different form, betraying the influence of the

[1] See Revillout's edition in R. Graffin et F. Nau, *Patrologia Orientalis*, tome ii (1907), pp. 185–98, and E. A. W. Budge, *Coptic Apocrypha in the Dialect of Upper Egypt*, 1913, pp. 179 ff.

[2] Migne, *Patr. Lat.*, vol. xxvi, col. 17. Gelasius and Bede, who also mention this spurious gospel, probably drew their information from Jerome.

[3] See G. Moesinger, *Vita et Martyrium Sancti Bartholomaei Apostoli ex sin-ceris fontibus Armeniacis in linguam Latinam conversa*, Salisburgi, 1877.

[4] See the edition (Oxford, 1886) by Sir E. A. W. Budge, who called my attention to this version of the legend. Assemani (*Bibl. Orient.* III. i. 317) says that the legend occurs frequently in Syriac manuscripts, but gives no details ; and inquiries from several Syriac scholars have failed to confirm his statement.

legend of Abgarus, King of Edessa. Before giving his version, it is as well to note that the legend can hardly have been known in Syriac-speaking lands before the ninth century. Otherwise it would surely have been worked into the Chronicle of Dionysius of Tell Maḥre (Patriarch of Antioch from A.D. 818 to 845). This writer [1] and Pseudo-Ephraim, [2] the author of the *Cave of the Treasures*, deal in great detail with the history of the treasures brought from Paradise. Adam took from the borders of Paradise gold, myrrh, and frankincense, and placed them in a cave, and blessed it, and consecrated it, so that it should be the house of prayer for him and for his sons, and called it the Cave of the Treasures. The Gnostic Apocalypse of Adam [3] connects these treasures definitely with the Magi: ' And we sealed this Testament, and placed it in the Cave of the Treasures, where it remains unto this day, with the treasures that Adam had taken from Paradise, the gold, the myrrh, and the incense. And the sons of the Magian kings shall come, shall take them, and shall bear them to the Son of God, in the grotto of Bethlehem of Judah.' [4]

To return to Solomon of Baṣra. He refers (p. 85) to the belief that the gifts brought by the Magi were descended from Adam only to condemn it as not received by the Church. The legend itself, as he gives it (p. 95), is briefly this. [5] Terah made these pieces for Abraham; Abraham gave them to Isaac; Isaac bought a village with them; the owner of the village carried them to Pharaoh; Pharaoh sent them to Solomon, who placed them round about the door of the altar. Nebuchadnezzar, struck by their beauty, carried them off. He gave them to some Persian youths who were at Babylon as hostages, and these youths, being released by Nebuchadnezzar, carried them to their parents. From Persia the Magi brought them with the other gifts. On their way, when near Edessa, the kings fell asleep by the wayside, and when they went on they left the coins behind. Certain merchants found them and brought them to the neighbourhood of Edessa. On that same day an angel appeared to the shepherds

[1] Cf. E. Renan, in *Journal Asiatique*, 1853, p. 467.

[2] C. Bezold, *Die Schatzhöhle*, 1883.

[3] Renan, *op. cit.*, p. 457.

[4] This passage is referred to in the Syriac ' Passing of the Blessed Virgin ' (W. Wright, *Contr. to the Apocr. Lit. of the New Testament*, 1865).

[5] The thirty pieces of silver, he says, were thirty pieces of silver according to the weight of the sanctuary (i.e. the sacred Jewish shekel of about 224 grains troy) and equivalent to 600 pieces according to the weight of his country (i.e. dirhems).

and gave them the seamless garment. The shepherds, taking this garment, met the merchants, and an exchange was made. The merchants went into Edessa with the garment, and the King Abgarus sent to them and asked if they had anything meet for kings, that he might buy it. When he saw the garment he asked whence they had it, and on learning the facts sent for the shepherds. Thus he acquired both the garment and the coins, and sent them to Christ for the good which He had done him in healing his sickness. Christ kept the garment but sent the pieces to the Jewish treasury. The priests gave them to Judas, and the rest follows as in the gospel.

I have said that this version differs considerably from that of Godfrey of Viterbo. Nevertheless there can be no doubt of their common origin ; they begin and end alike ; the seamless garment is associated with the coins in the same mysterious way.[1] Godfrey's Armenian astrologer corresponds to King Abgarus. But we miss the attractive episode of the presentation of the coins to the infant Christ and the losing of them by the Virgin.

Of course the discovery of other Syriac versions may throw new light on the development of the legend. But with the present evidence we are probably justified in supposing that the ultimate source of both Godfrey's and Solomon's stories would be found in a comparatively simple form in Pseudo-Bartholomew. Possibly the minute germ from which the connexion of the coins with the Magi sprang is to be found in the well-known Apocryphal Gospel of Matthew. The date of this apocryph is not later than the fourth century after Christ. Here in chapter xvi [2] we read : ' then they opened their treasures, and gave exceeding great gifts to Mary and Joseph. *But to the Child Himself they each offered one gold coin.* After these, one offered gold, the second frankincense, and the third myrrh.'

Surely there is an echo of this in Godfrey's stanza :

Hos reges Saba quos post nova stella vocavit
ferre Deo nummos Veterum scriptura notavit,
cum tria tres socii dona tulere magi.

[1] In the German poem of King Orendel, which dates from the second half of the twelfth century, the King buys the seamless vesture from the Fisherman for thirty gold pennies, brought to him from Our Lady by Gabriel. But although the poem says that this was the sum for which Judas betrayed his Lord, I do not find it assumed, as Creizenach has suggested it is, that these were actually the same fateful coins. See Simrock's translation of the poem (1845), pp. 32–4.

[2] Tischendorf, *Ev. Apocr.*, 1876, p. 83.

The picturesque effect of these three coins would appeal to the mythopœic faculty. It would be easy to multiply them by ten. And once connected with the Magi, with all the mysterious traditions that involved the Kings of the East, it would be but natural to take the history of the coins back to the time when the Sabaean land previously played a part in Biblical history, i.e. to the time of the Queen of Sheba. Possibly also the tradition that the Magi were descended from Abraham by Keturah [1] may have made it easy to carry the story of the coins back as far as Abraham.

This, however, is mere speculation. Let us return to the legend itself.[2]

In the third quarter of the fourteenth century a great vogue was given to the story by two writers, Ludolph of Suchem and John of Hildesheim. The latter, a Carmelite friar, is better known, but the priority seems to rest with Ludolph. His *de Itinere Terrae Sanctae* [3] was dedicated to Baldwin of Steinfort, Bishop of Paderborn, a fact which dates it before 1361. Internal evidence and comparison with the ' Book of Cologne ' show that it is later than 1350. Ludolph, according to his own statement, was in the Holy Land from 1336 to 1341.

He gives as his authority (chapter xxxix) the *History of the Kings of the East*.[4] The coins were some of a number made for Ninus by Terah, who received thirty of them *pro suo salario*, a pleasing touch. Abraham spent them in his exile, and they came into the hands of the Ishmaelites. The Ishmaelites bought Joseph with them, and with them Joseph's brethren bought corn out of Egypt. Afterwards they were sent into the land of

---

[1] Did this tradition originate in the name *Sheba* borne by one of the grandchildren of Abraham by Keturah ? (Gen. xxv. 3.)

[2] For completeness sake, though I have no details, I note here that in connexion with Godfrey's version of the legend Creizenach (*Judas Iscarioth in Legende und Sage des Mittelalters*, in *Beiträge zur Gesch. d. deutschen Sprache u. Lit.* ii (1876), p. 179) mentions a Catalan version, supposed to belong to the time of Raymond Lully (who died 1315). See *Jahrbuch für roman. u. engl. Lit.* v, p. 137 note.

[3] Ed. F. Deycks, *Stuttgarter Lit. Verein*, 1851. Compare the same critic's *Ueber ältere Pilgerfahrten*, 58 ff. He regards John of Hildesheim as the source of Ludolph ; but the view taken in the text, and supported by Neumann in *Archives de l'Orient Latin*, ii (1884), Doc. 313 ff., seems to be dictated by the chronological data. Ludolph's work has been translated for the Palestine Pilgrims Text Society (1895).

[4] As Ludolph was in the Holy Land for some time, he may very possibly have gone to some Syriac sources.

Saba to buy merchandise for Pharaoh (*in Saba pro mercimoniis ex parte Pharaonis*). The Queen of Sheba brought them to Solomon, and they were placed in the Temple ; thence they were carried off by Nebuchadnezzar, who gave them to the King of Godolia.[1] There they remained until, at the time of the birth of Christ, the kingdom of Godolia was transferred to the kingdom of Nubia. Melchior brought them to Christ, because older and nobler gold than this he found none in his treasury. They were lost by Mary when she fled to Egypt in the Balsam Garden ; and there they were found by a certain shepherd, who kept them until the time of the Passion approached. Falling ill and hearing of the works of Christ, this shepherd came to Him and was cured. The rest of the story agrees with the account as given in Godfrey of Viterbo ; but there is no excursus on the sacred garment, nor are we told what the coins were like. The discrepancy between the metals is briefly explained. Finally we are told that when the predestined object of the denarii was fulfilled, they were immediately separated and dispersed.

Ludolph's book was meant for pilgrims and those interested in their journeys. John of Hildesheim appealed to an audience perhaps even wider. His *Liber de gestis ac trina beatissimorum trium regum translacione* was dedicated to and written at the bidding of Florentius of Wevelinghoven or Wevelkoven, Bishop of Münster. Florentius held that see from 1364 to 1379, and, as John died at Marienau in 1375, the date of the composition is fixed between 1364 and 1375. It appeared in a German translation as early as 1389.[2] In modern times attention was called to it by Goethe.

The account given by John in chapters xxviii, xxix, is

---

[1] I cannot explain Godolia and Godolias (see below), unless they are echoes of Gedaliah, son of Ahikam, who, having been made governor by Nebuchadnezzar over the people who were left in Judaea after the destruction of Jerusalem, ruled for two months and was then murdered (Jer. xl, xli, and 2 Kings xxv. 22–5). The LXX, Josephus and the Vulgate call him Godolias. The connexion with Nebuchadnezzar seems to favour this explanation. In John of Hildesheim (see below) Godolia is the name of Balthasar's kingdom.

[2] The Latin version was first printed in Germany in 1477 ; reprinted in 1478, 1481, 1486, and 1514, and at Modena (as *Legenda sanctorum trium regum*) in 1490. A more or less critical edition was published by E. Köpke from a Brandenburg manuscript in *Mittheil. aus d. Handschr. d. Ritterakad. zu Brandenburg*, 1878. A text with very full *apparatus criticus* accompanies the edition of the English version in the Early English Text Society's publication, *The Three Kings of Cologne*, ed. by C. Horstmann (1886), to which I may refer the reader for further details.

very full. I have space to note only the chief points [of interest.

The source of the story of the offering of the coins by Melchior is described as the *libri Indorum*.[1] After the death of Jacob, Joseph sent the coins to the kingdom of Saba for spices to bury his father, and they were placed in the treasury of the Sabaean kings. Then, just as Godfrey and Ludolph relate, they found their way to the Temple of Jerusalem. In the time of Rehoboam, in the taking of Jerusalem and the spoiling of the Temple, they came into the hands of the King of the Arabians, who was then an ally of the Egyptians, and thus into the royal treasury of Arabia. Melchior, King of Nubia and of the Arabians, brought, together with many other precious gifts, these thirty denarii, since older and nobler gold in his treasury he found none. These only he offered to our Lord, passing over the other gifts in his fear (as described in chapter xxii). The treasures (i.e. the coins, frankincense, and myrrh) were taken by the Virgin, wrapped up in a linen cloth, and lost on her flight into Egypt. They were found by a Bedouin shepherd. He kept them until, shortly before the Passion, he fell into an incurable disease. Hearing of the fame of Jesus, he came to Him, and was cured and converted. He offered the gifts to Jesus ; but Jesus knew them and bade him put them on the altar. And the priest burnt the frankincense, and put the myrrh with the coins in the treasury. In order that all the Jews indifferently should be responsible for the Passion and death of Christ, the priests took the coins out of the common treasury and gave them to Judas. Part of the myrrh was mixed with the vinegar offered to Christ on the cross, and the rest was given by Nicodemus for the embalming of the body. The coins when returned by Judas were divided, as we have learned they were from Godfrey and Ludolph. A description follows of the cemetery in the Potter's Field ; also we have Godfrey's ingenious explanation of the discrepancy between Gospel and legend as to the metal of the coins, given in a more elaborate and confused form. They were called by the general name *argentei*, just as gold denarii are now called *scuti mutones*[2] or florins. The type, weight, and appearance of the coins in use

[1] Doubtless, as Horstmann suggests, John's sources may have been largely fictitious ; in any case he can hardly have known such Oriental sources except through some Latin history.

[2] In the Modena edition *scudati mutenes*. The French *écus* with the *mouton* (*Agnus Dei*) are meant.

from the time of Abraham down to the destruction of Jerusalem by Titus and Vespasian remained, we are assured, unchanged, and in all parts of the East coins never alter their weight or value. Then comes an obscure passage on the garment of Christ : the style and size of the seamless garment have remained in hereditary use among very many princes and nobles down to the writer's day.[1] Each of the thirty pieces is said to be worth about three florins ;[2] and on one side of the coin is impressed the head of a king, laureate, and on the other side are Chaldaic letters which modern men cannot read or decipher.

The early German translation of John's book already mentioned[3] presents certain small variations, of which perhaps the only one worth recording is that Potiphar, Pharaoh's chamberlain, is said to have bought Joseph directly from his brethren with these coins.

It will be observed that John differs from the other writers in saying that the Egyptians, not Nebuchadnezzar, carried off the coins in the reign of Rehoboam, i. e. when Shishak took Jerusalem.

The legend seems to have found its way into England in the fourteenth century, although it has left, so far as I know, but one slight trace at that early date. This occurs in a mutilated scripture history, which used to be attributed to Adam Davie (*circa* A.D. 1312). But the attribution is baseless, and there is, it would seem, no reason why this fragment should not belong to the end of the fourteenth century. In that case the author may have learned the story from Ludolph or John of Hildesheim. The fragment is as follows :[4]

> For þritty pens þai solde*n* þat childe ; þe seller hiȝth Judas.
> Þo Ruben com hom *and* myssed hy*m* ; sori ynouȝ he was.
> Þe childes kirtel hij nome*n* ; *and in* blood it wou*n*de
> Ac caste*n* it at her fader feet ; *and* seide*n* hou þai it fou*n*de.
> Allas allas seide Jacob ; þat I þis day schulde ywite.
> Wilde bestes in þe wood ; habbeþ my childe y-bite.

---

[1] The garment, we have seen, is also associated with the coins by Godfrey and Solomon. The object here appears to be to draw a parallel between the fashion in dress and the fashion in the coinage in respect of permanence.

[2] Say 25*s*. of our money.

[3] See Simrock, *Die Legende von den heiligen drei Königen*.

[4] MS. Laud Misc. 622, fol. 65 (Bodleian Library). I have to thank Mr. A. E. Cowley for procuring me a copy of the whole of this portion of the manuscript. W. Sandys (*Christmas Carols*, 1833, p. lxxxv) notes the connexion of the verses with the legend.

Unfortunately the verses that should follow are lost ; but it is possible that there was no further allusion to the legend than that involved in the alteration of the price from twenty to thirty pence.

A fifteenth-century manuscript account in the British Museum (34276, fol. 33 b), written in Latin by an English scribe of the name of Barow, is obviously an abridgement of the story as told by John of Hildesheim. It was probably taken, to judge from the style of the writing, not from the printed book, but from one of the many earlier manuscripts. It omits the stages by which the coins, after they were deposited in the Temple, came into the hands of the Magi. The *Badwini* (Bedouins) of John of Hildesheim are transformed into the English-sounding name *Bodwyny*.[1] The explanation of the discrepancy between the metals is omitted, but the passage describing the coins agrees almost *verbatim* with John. This writer adds :[2] after the denarii had fulfilled that which was to be fulfilled, they were dispersed.

The pilgrim Felix Fabri, of Nuremberg, at the end of the fifteenth century, read the story, he tells us, in a certain long and wordy history.[3] He is not given to brevity himself, but his words accurately describe John of Hildesheim's work. Nevertheless, certain small coincidences show that he rather followed Ludolph, or Ludolph's source. Thus he says that the coins were sent to the land of Saba *pro mercimoniis*, without mentioning spices ; Nebuchadnezzar presented them to Godolias,[4] by whom they were transmitted to the kingdom of Nubia. He does not mention the balsam-garden ; the treasures were lost in the desert. But from the finding of them by 'a certain shepherd' down to the end of the story he agrees most closely with Ludolph, except that he does not deal with the question of the metal, and that he supposes all the thirty to have been spent on the purchase of the Potter's Field.

It seems clear from the evidence here given that between

[1] The manuscript of John's work at Corpus Christi College, Cambridge, has *Bodewini*. The English manuscripts edited by Horstmann do not attempt to describe the shepherd's race.

[2] Like Ludolph, and like the English translation (Horstmann, pp. 100, 101).

[3] See his *Evagatorium*, i. 426 (ed. by C. D. Hassler in *Stuttgarter Lit. Verein*, 1846-9). The Palestine Pilgrims Text Society has published the work in English (1892-3). The passage in ques tion is translated by M. de Vogüé in *Rev. des Deux Mondes*, viii (1875), 531 f. ; see also Barbier de Montault in *Rev. de l'Art Chrétien*, N.S. iv (1886), in an article to be referred to later.

[4] Godolia, in Ludolph and in John of Hildesheim (chapter xi), is the name of the kingdom ; but John does not men tion it in this connexion. See above, p. 97.

Godfrey of Viterbo and Ludolph of Suchem there is a gap which should be filled by the *History of the Kings of the East* from which, or from different versions of which, both Ludolph and John of Hildesheim drew.

There are two other manuscripts in the British Museum which represent different versions of the legend. Both are of the fifteenth century. One (22553, fol. 144 b) is in an Italian hand. I mention here only the more important details in which the account differs from those already described. Nothing is said about the coins being of gold. Abraham bought with them the tomb in which Adam and Eve had been buried. From the Egyptian treasury they came into the hands of Moses, who gave them to a Queen of Sheba. The Virgin, when she had received them from the Magi, gave them to the shepherds who came to adore Christ, because they were poor ; and they departing placed them in the Temple. There is no reference to the division of the money between the soldiers and the purchase of the Potter's Field.

The other manuscript (34139, fol. 87), which is in a German hand, differs from the preceding in stating that the coins found their way into the Temple for the second time as the price for which the Virgin redeemed her Son according to the law, after she had presented Him in the Temple. Finally, I may note an isolated statement in the thirteenth-century *City of Jerusalem* to the effect that the thirty pieces were struck at Capernaum. This does not seem to fit in with any of the versions of the legend that we have considered.[1]

In all the above versions, except that of Solomon of Baṣra, the coins are actually presented by the Magi to the infant Christ. Solomon, by a very complicated process, brings the coins into the hands of King Abgarus. In Godfrey's version also there is some confusion in the transition from the finding of the coins by the shepherds to their acquisition by Abgarus's double, the Armenian astrologer. It looks as if, in the story from which both Godfrey and Solomon drew, this point was not quite clear. Solomon has ' joined his flats ' better than Godfrey, but has evidently had to exercise considerable ingenuity in doing so.

If I may be allowed to venture one more hypothesis, I would

[1] The *City of Jerusalem*, part ii, in no. 8 of the Palestine Pilgrims Text Society's publications, p. 31. The date of this work appears to be between A.D. 1220 and 1229.

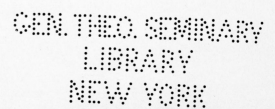

suggest that the two short versions in which the whole episode of the losing and finding of the coins is omitted may, in view of their comparative simplicity, represent a very old form of the story.

To quite a different group of legends from those already mentioned belongs one which is incorporated in the curious History of the Holy Rood-tree;[1] the manuscript which contains this story is of the third quarter of the twelfth century, and thus contemporary with Godfrey of Viterbo. But this story did not become so popular as the one which we have described above. Briefly it is this: the three miraculous rods of Moses which eventually became the Holy Cross were planted by David; they grew up into a tree, and each year for thirty years David marked the trunk with a silver hoop of thirty pounds, which was forged round it. When the tree was cut down to make a beam (which, however, was not used) for Solomon's Temple, the thirty silver hoops were made into thirty plates and hung in the Temple by the king for his father's soul. ' That was the same silver for which the wretched Judas betrayed our Lord to death ', for the Jews took these thirty pieces and gave them to him.

In a Greek Legend of the Holy Cross[2] the rings of silver do not go back as far as David; but it is said that after the beam was found to be unsuitable for the Temple, Solomon, learning from the Erythraean Sibyl its sacred destiny, set it upright, and fastened round it thirty ' crowns ' of pure silver; and these crowns it was that Judas afterwards received.

P. Leopoldo de Feis[3] has some ingenious speculations concerning this legend, which when he wrote he knew only in the form published by Sir E. M. Thompson. The silver hoops remind him of the ' thirty " crowns "'[4] commemorating for Christians the same number of denarii of Judas', which Anthony of Novgorod in A.D. 1200 saw above the ciborium of St. Sophia. It is indeed possible that the legend was inspired by the sight

[1] Published by A. S. Napier, Early Eng. Text Soc., 1894 (pp. 24, 25). Napier also gives (p. 69) the Latin version of the Judas story from a late twelfth-century manuscript at Jesus College, Oxford, and refers to the later manuscripts. (Cf. Sir E. M. Thompson, *Journ. Brit. Archaeol. Assoc.* xxxvii, 1881, pp. 241 f.) Mr. Robin Flower called my attention to this legend, and to

the Greek one mentioned in the next note.

[2] Gretser, *Hortus Crucis*, Ingolstadt, 1610, p. 233.

[3] *Le Monete del Prezzo di Giuda*, p. 7 (Florence, 1902; extr. from *Studi religiosi*).

[4] It is to be noted that the Greek legend quoted above calls the hoops crowns (στέφανοι).

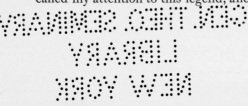

of thirty such rings. Feis further remarks, in connexion with the fact that the legend does not regard the thirty pieces of silver as coined money, but as rings of wrought metal, that primitive currency frequently took the form of rings ; the Hebrew word for talent, for instance, *kikkar*, means a circular thing.[1] One may doubt, however, whether the maker of the legend, even in its most primitive form, had any conception of this.

Finally, an incidental reference in a thirteenth-century manuscript continuation of William of Tyre[2] seems to point to some other source than those which we have enumerated : At Acco there is also a tower called the Accursed, situate upon the wall which surrounds the city, which, if the vulgar opinion deserve credit, took its name because the silver pieces for which the traitor Judas sold the Lord are said to have been made there.

Here we may leave the legend. Perhaps the somewhat irritating gaps in the material so far collected may stimulate some scholar, better equipped than myself, to bridge them over. But it is not amiss to recall the warning which I seem to have heard somewhere : he who thinks that he has attained a definitive result in tracing the development of a mediaeval legend may deceive himself, but he will not deceive his readers.

But the history of the coins does not stop here, and we have now to deal with something less elusive in the shape of those pieces which, each professing to be a ' Judas-penny ', found their way into the sanctuaries of Christendom.

So far, more than thirty such pieces have been recorded ; some are still extant ; others though lost have been described with sufficient accuracy to enable us to say to what class they belong ; of others we have but a bare mention. What we do know makes it probable that no single one of the professed relics[3] was actually a coin of the kind that was in circulation in Judaea in the time of Christ.[4]

[1] Possibly, however, circular like a round cake, not a ring.

[2] Brit. Mus. Royal 14 C x, fol. 264. I owe the reference to Mr. Herbert.

[3] I use the word ' relic ' in its most general sense, not necessarily implying that all these coins were the object of a cult.

[4] On the general subject of coins as relics I may refer to E. Babelon, *Traité des Monnaies*, i. 76 f., and my article in Hastings's *Dict. of Religion and Ethics*, vol. iii, pp. 703 f. See also the pamphlet of Feis quoted above (p. 102), p. 3, note 2. The interesting *nummus perforatus lancea Sancti Mauricii Martyris* which used to be at Canterbury (J. Dart, *History of the Cathedral Church of Canterbury*, 1726, App. xlvii ; from Brit. Mus. MS. Cotton, Galba E iv, fol. 125 b, of the early fourteenth century) was possibly a coin of *Mauricius Tiberius*.

The most exhaustive treatment of this subject is to be found in an article by the distinguished ' lipsanographer ', M. F. de Mély.[1]   This was, however, preceded in 1886 by an article by M. Barbier de Montault,[2] dealing especially with the reliquary of S. Croce in Gerusalemme.   Finally, some additional information has been furnished by three other writers.[3]   The existence of these articles relieves me from overloading these pages with detailed references for each coin.

/M. de Mély has noted the following six places in which specimens of the Thirty Pieces, not sufficiently described to allow of identification, were preserved :

(1) The Visitandines at Aix.
(2) Notre Dame du Puy.
(3) The Abbey of St. Denis.
(4) Montserrat in Catalonia.
(5) S. Croce in Florence.
(6) The Annunziata in Florence.

To these Feis adds (7) yet another, which was in the now no longer existing Church of S. Maria dei Candeli in Florence.[4]

Of the coin at S. Croce we are told that Cosimo de' Medici the Elder received it from the Greek Patriarch who came to the Florentine Council (*scil*. in 1439–42).   Richa, who says that the coin in the Annunziata was similar to it, suspends judgement as to the authenticity of the S. Croce relic, which he says was neither a Hebrew nor a Roman coin.   The piece in Notre Dame du Puy was left to the ancestors of the barony of Agrain by a virtuous lady of that house, who, having a son in the service of the Grand Turk, received from him this precious denarius, ' which is of great efficacy for the comforting of women labouring with child '.   As to the pieces at Aix and St. Denis, M. de Villenoisy points out that, as they are only mentioned in the *Dictionnaire des Reliques* of Collin de Plancy, an author who is not to be trusted

---

[1] *Les Deniers de Judas dans la Tradition du Moyen Âge* in the *Revue Numismatique*, 1899, pp. 500–9

[2] *Rev. de l'Art Chrétien*, N.S., iv. 214 f.

[3] F. de Villenoisy, *Le Denier de Judas du Couvent des Capucins d'Enghien* (Enghien, 1900) ; P. Perdrizet, *Une Recherche à faire à Rosas* in *Revue des Études Anc.* 1902 ; and especially P. Leopoldo de Feis, *Le Monete del Prezzo di Giuda* (see above, p. 102, note 3).   My thanks are due to MM. de Villenoisy and Perdrizet for copies of their contributions.   I must also acknowledge my indebtedness to the late Mr. F. W. Hasluck for numerous references to other literature bearing on the subject.

[4] Feis, *loc. cit.*, p. 5.

when he does not give his sources, they cannot be regarded as undoubted examples.

Finally, I am informed by Professor Markoff, through M. Alexeieff, that a silver coin is preserved as one of the thirty at (8) the Abbey of the Trinity and St. Sergius in Moscow. Professor Markoff characterizes it as an evident forgery, but does not describe it. Another undescribed piece (9) is, I am informed on the same authority, preserved in the monastery of Souprasl near Bielostock.

The next group consists of coins of which the description is known.

Fig. 63.—Silver coins of Rhodes, fifth-fourth century B.C. (British Museum).

Of these, no less than eight can be identified, either because they are still extant, or from illustrations or descriptions, as coins of *Rhodes*. For the most part, it would seem, they date from the fourth century before Christ. They bear on the obverse a facing head of the Sun-god, with flowing hair, sometimes surrounded by rays ; on the reverse is a rose and the inscription POΔION. Fig. 63 shows specimens of two coins of the same class now in the British Museum. The coin which was in the Temple at Paris must, from Morand's description, have been a coin of the same issue as one in the British Museum,[1] for it had the same mint-letter (Δ) and adjunct (thunderbolt).

The places where these Rhodian coins were or are preserved are the following :

(10) Rhodes, in the castle of the Knights of St. John. The earliest mention of this particular piece which I have been able

---

[1] Brit. Mus. Catal. of Greek Coins, *Caria*, p. 233, no. 26.

to find is by Luchino dal Campo,[1] who wrote the account of the visit of Niccolò III of Este to the Holy Land in 1413. He describes it as ' one of those very denarii of silver for which Christ was sold ; the which denarius is of the size of an *agruntano*.[2] On one side is the head in relief and on the other is a flower as it were like the flower of a marguerite '.

As the Rhodian piece is not mentioned in the account of the voyage of the Seigneur d'Anglure,[3] who visited the island in 1395, or by the Metz pilgrim in 1396, it is probable that the relic was only acquired between 1396 and 1413. It is unlikely that the Judas-penny would have been passed over, when the *denier de Sainte Hélène* was mentioned.[4]

[1] *Viaggio a Gerusalemme di Niccolò da Este*, ed. by G. Ghinassi in *Collezione di opere ined. o rare pubbl. per cura della R. Comm. pe' Testi di Lingua nelle Prov. dell' Emilia*, i (Turin, 1861), p. 143.

[2] The editor suggests that this word is a mistake for *agostaro* (Augustale, the gold coin issued by Frederick II). But this was hardly in circulation in the fifteenth century, so that dal Campo would not be likely to use it as a measure of size.

[3] Bonnardot et Longnon, *Le Saint Voyage de Jhérusalem du Seigneur d'Anglure* (Soc. des anc. Textes français, 1878).

[4] *Op. cit.*, p. 9 : ' item, ung des deniers de saincte Helene envaissellé en plomb, sur lequel on fait les bullettes de Rodes qui sont de si grant vertu ; et les fait on le jour du Grant Vendredi.' Cf. p. 94, note : ' Item, en laidicte esglise de Saint Jehan nous fuit montrés ung dez denier d'ors l'amperise saincte Eslainne, qui est aissis en ung pomelz de laiton et soldéz di plont, car aultrement ne se lait ledit denier asseoir ne solder. Sor lequelz denier on fait chescun ans plussour bullete de virge sire, c'est aissavoir le jour dou Saint Vanredi, en tant que on dit l'office en l'esglise ; lezquelle bullete porteet on plussour vertus belle et noble.' The anonymous pilgrim from Metz in 1396 saw the ' denier d'or à l'effigie de sainte Helène, soudé en plomb à un pommier de laiton,

dont on prend des empreintes en cire vierge à l'office du saint vendredi ', &c. See *L'Austrasie*, vol. ii (Metz), 1838, p. 234. We shall see later on the bearing of these passages on our investigation. It may be noted that Cennino Cennini in his treatise on painting has a chapter (188, p. 177, in Mrs. Herringham's translation) on ' how to make impressions of *santelene* in wax or paste'. *Sancta Helena* was a very general term for any Byzantine coin of late date, especially for the more blundered and less artistic specimens. They may have got the name from the cross which so many of them bore. Hasluck (in *Essays and Studies presented to William Ridgeway*, Cambridge, 1913, p. 636) identifies them with solidi of the ninth or tenth centuries showing busts or figures of two emperors flanking a cross, in the same way as the eikon type of Constantine and Helena represents the two saints side by side supporting the True Cross between them. Compare the ' escudeletto de Sto. Heleno ', a cup-shaped Byzantine coin used as a charm (*Rev. Numism.*, 1908, p. 137, where Peiresc is quoted as reporting that such coins were given by the Penitents of Aix to condemned criminals). Enormous quantities of Byzantine solidi were certainly pierced and worn as amulets. See Ducange, *Diss. de Inferioris Aevi Numism.*, c. lxxviii (lxix), who quotes Bosius on the value of coins of St. Helen as a remedy against epilepsy.

After Luchino dal Campo comes Brunner (1470)[1] and then Johann Tucher of Nuremberg, who went to the Holy Land in 1479 and 1480. He mentions the coin in his description of Rhodes, and again, when dealing with the Potter's Field, he says, ' I have seen one of these pennies, and three such in silver are worth a ducat '.[2]

Felix Fabri, after telling the story as we have already heard him, continues: 'After the purchase of the field they were dispersed throughout all the world; I saw one at Rhodes, of which Johann Tucher of Nuremberg made an impression. He made a model in lead and cast similar ones in silver, which he distributed to his friends. In the year 1485, when we were assembled at Nuremberg to hold the provincial chapter, the said person gave one of these denarii to each of the brothers. The size is the same as that of the cross-blafferts,[3] and on one side is the face of a man

They were widely used for this purpose; for instance, Girolamo Dandini reports the use of this remedy in Crete (*Missione apost.*, Cesena, 1656, p. 14; I quote the French transl., *Voyage du Mont Liban*, Paris, 1675, p. 18): ' mais ce qui est bien plus surprenant & au dessus des forces de la nature, c'est une monnoye qu'on nomme de sainte Helene, & qu'on trouve dans les campagnes dont il y en a de cuivre & d'autre d'argent. L'on pretend que cette Sainte se rencontrant en ce pays-là sans argent fit faire de la monnoye de cuir, qui se changea en metal en la distribuant. Cette monnoye a encore aujourd'huy la vertu de guerir du mal caduc ceux qui la tiennent dans leur main ou l'appliquent sur leur chair '. Finally, I may cite a Bulgarian legend which gives a quaint account of the origin and use of the *santelene*, although that term is not used to describe them. When the great cross was cut up, the sawdust and little pieces were collected in a cloth. The king (Constantine) mixed them with gold and silver, melted all down together and caused to be struck pieces of gold and silver money with the images of Constantine and Helena, and the Cross between them. These coins were presented to the Christian children whom it had been

proposed to kill in order to cure the king with their blood. The coins of Constantine and Helena performed miracles, curing the sick and especially children on whom a spell had been cast. These coins were hollowed like little saucers so as to hold water, and this water was used to give drink to the sick and wash them We have these coins to the present day, and children are washed in this manner (Lydia Schischmánoff, *Légendes religieuses bulgares*, Paris, 1896, pp. 74–5). It should be observed that the cup-shaped or scyphate fabric of the coins is original, being produced by convex and concave dies, and not due to subsequent alteration for the purpose described. The popularity of these *santelene* can hardly have originated, as has been suggested, when a treasure of them was found at Rome in 1398, as recorded by Thomas Walsingham; the references given above show that they were objects of much veneration in 1395, and doubtless long before.

[1] *Zeitschr. d. deutsch. Palästina-Vereins*, xxix (1906), p. 25.

[2] Feyerabend, *Bewehrtes Reyssbuch* (1659), 656, 666.

[3] *Quantitas est sicut blaphordorum crucis*, which M. de Vogüé ingeniously translates ' il y en a autant que de clous

and on the other is a lily. There was certainly an inscription, but it cannot now be seen.' Fabri mentions the coin at Rhodes (in the Castle) when he comes (iii. 288) to describe the relics in that island. ' Marguerite ' and ' lily ' are not very good descriptions of the Rhodian rose, but will pass muster for the time.

Hans Tucher kept a reproduction of the coin in his collection, which consisted mainly of Roman portrait-coins : ' an example or cast of one of the thirty pence, for which Christ the Lord was sold, as indeed I Hans Tucher the elder have seen of this same penny two alike, namely one at Rhodes and the other at Bethlehem at the guardian's, both which were shown to me as true ones. Three of the pence are worth in silver an Hungarian gulden or a ducat.'[1]

Conrad Grünemberg of Constanz, who went to the Holy Land in 1486, saw the relic and had a reproduction made by a Netherlandish goldsmith.[2]

Yet another reference to the Rhodian piece is to be found in Bernhard of Breydenbach's *Peregrinationes ad Terram Sanctam* (Mainz, 1486) in the chapter on the relics at Rhodes : ' item ibi illorum xxx. argenteorum denariorum unus esse perhibetur, ymmo et demonstratur, pro quibus Iudas vendidit Christum iudeis '.

References indeed are plentiful at this time, and we may pass over several dating from 1485 to 1488, and come to that which we find in the *Stabilimenta* of Guill. Caoursin.[3] In describing the veneration which should be paid to the relics, he says : ' nor let less honour be paid to the silver denarius, one of those thirty pieces of silver at which the traitor Judas priced Christ : from an impression of which stamps are made in white wax every year while the Passion is being chanted by the priest ; which stamps are esteemed to be of virtue for the health of men, for the labour of women, and for perils by sea.'

As we find a similar relic described as being in the possession of the Order at Malta, we may presume that when the knights left Rhodes in 1523 they brought this precious coin with them.

à la croix '. I do not know how he arrived at this interpretation. *Blaphordus* or *blaffardus* is the German *Blaffert* or *Plappert*, a silver coin widely current in Germany and Switzerland in Fabri's time. A variety with a cross on it was called *Kreuzblaffert, blaphordus crucis.*

[1] *Mitt. des Vereins f. Gesch. d. Stadt Nürnberg* (1895), quoted in *Monatsblatt der Num. Ges. in Wien*, ix (1913), p. 108.
[2] R. Röhricht u. H. Meisner, *Deutsche Pilgerreisen* (1880), p. 154.
[3] *Stabilimenta Rhodiorum Militum Sacri ordinis* (1496), fol. d 1 *verso*.

The Prior of the Order, Ant. Cressin (1556–84), used to distribute to pilgrims wax impressions covered with silver or gold leaf.

(11) Rome, in S. Croce in Gerusalemme. This piece is still kept in a little fifteenth-century reliquary inscribed with the name of Cardinal Bernardin de Carvajal, and given by him towards the end of the fifteenth century.[1]

(12) Rosas in Catalonia (still preserved).

(13) Oviedo, in the Camera Santa of S. Salvadore.

(14) Paris, Church of St. John Lateran.

(15) Paris, Temple.

(16) Vincennes.

(17) Enghien, still preserved in the Capuchin Convent, and formerly at Héverlé near Louvain. It had been acquired by the Celestines of Héverlé after the death of the Marquise Marie-Madeleine de Hamal (wife of Guillaume de Croy, who died in 1521); she had acquired it at Rome. This is a Rhodian four-drachm piece with the magistrate's name ΑΡΙΣΤΟΚΡΙΤΟΣ.[2] M. de Villenoisy describes the adjunct as an ' armed man '. Curiously enough this adjunct is not, to my knowledge, otherwise associated with Aristokritos, who generally, if not always, placed an *aplustre* on the coins struck by his authority.

(18) Another specimen with the same magistrate's name (ΑΡΙΣΤΟΚΡΙΤΟΣ) was formerly in the Church of S. Francesco dei Riformati at Spezia. Its true character, as a Rhodian coin, was discovered by a scholar in 1787.[3] Considering the innumerable varieties of the Rhodian coinage, the existence of two coins of Aristokritos among these relics is remarkable, unless one was a reproduction of the other.

(19) Bethlehem : seen by Hans Tucher (see above).

Rouille, in his *Promptuaire des Médailles*,[4] gives, together with

---

[1] See especially B. de Montault, *loc. cit.* I have not been able to consult his *Antiquités chrétiennes de Rome*, in which the reliquary is photographed. M. de Mély gives a sketch. Mr. A. H. S. Yeames calls my attention to a passage in the manuscript Travels of R. Sharp (Brit. Mus. Sloane MS. 1522): on May 15, 1701, he says, ' We went to Ghigies Palace [Palazzo Chigi in Rome] and saw a shekel of the sanctuary which the man told me was worth a Roman crown and a half, one of the 30 pieces of money which Judas received for our Saviour, which hath something like this [rude attempt at a rose] on one side and a face on the other '. It looks as if Sharp had in his memoranda confused the Chigi Palace with S. Croce.

[2] Cf. B. V. Head, British Museum Catal. of Greek Coins, *Caria*, p. 241, no. 122. Feis has failed to recognize that the Héverlé and Enghien pieces are identical.

[3] Feis, p. 5.

[4] Lyon, 1553, part ii. 10.

an imaginary medallic portrait of Judas, a reproduction of one of the Rhodian coins. The engraver has made the Δ of POΔION into an A (fig. 64).

(20) Another Greek coin which was utilized for this pious purpose was one of the famous silver ten-drachm pieces of Syracuse, struck at the end of the fifth or beginning of the fourth century B.C. On the reverse was a chariot-group, below which were the prize arms competed for in the Assinarian games. On the obverse was the female head now generally identified as Arethusa ; behind it a small shell by which we are enabled to identify the exact variety. The specimen, which has since unfortunately

Fig. 64.—Medallic portrait of Judas Iscariot, and reproduction of a Rhodian coin, from Rouille's *Promptuaire des Médailles*.

disappeared, and of which the provenance was never known, was framed in a gold mount and inscribed in Gothic letters *Quia precium sanguinis est*.[1]

(21) An ancient barbarous Celtic imitation of a silver tetradrachm of Philip II of Macedon, with a head of Zeus on the obverse, and a mounted jockey on the reverse, may next be mentioned ; this was mounted in a silver disc which bears the engraved inscription, of about 1700 : ' Das Ist Der Rechten Silberlinge Einer Davor Christus Verkauft Worten.'[2]

(22) Still preserved in the treasury of the Cathedral of Sens, and mentioned in an inventory of 1464, is a silver *dirhem* of the Egyptian Sultan El-Ashraf Salaḥ-al-din Khalil, of the Baḥri Mamluks (A.D. 1290–3).[3]

(23) M. de Mély refers incidentally to the coins once

[1] Matthew xxvii. 6. It is described in Rollin and Feuardent's *Catalogue d'une Coll. de Médailles*, Paris, 1864, p. 124, no. 1769, where it is wrongly called an octodrachm.

[2] *Daheim*, 1906, no. 43, p. 20. The writer says that it was sent to him from Silesia.

[3] Cf. de Montault, p. 218, who quotes from a seventeenth-century inventory.

preserved in the church of S. Eustorgio at Milan ; but he does
not give them a place in his list.   Ughelli, however, to whom he
refers, describes them as *monetae quaedam ex iis, quas Christo
Magos tributi nomine obtulisse pie credunt*.[1]   The legends which
we have discussed above show that these coins may perhaps be
classed with the ' Thirty Pieces '.   Later authorities speak only
of a single gold coin, which as a matter of fact was a solidus of the
Emperor Zeno (A.D. 474–91).   It was known as the *ducato dei tre
Magi*.   Allegranza suggested that the remains of the three kings
had been translated to Milan in the reign of Zeno, and a coin
of his reign placed in the coffin from which it was afterwards
extracted.   This, however, is a pure conjecture.   All that is
certain is that this solidus was exposed for the public worship
as one of the gold coins offered to Christ by the Magi.[2]

Finally, Feis has been able to add, at one stroke, no less than
nine more specimens (24–32), for he cites Ant. Masini (*Bologna
perlustrata*, 1650, p. 51) as evidence that, in SS. Trinità di
S. Stefano in Bologna, one of the shekels for which Judas sold
Christ was placed on each of the nine columns which support
the high altar.   From the description which Masini gives it is
clear that these were specimens (or reproductions) of the Jewish
shekels attributed by some authorities to Simon Maccabaeus,
by others to the First Revolt against Rome (see above, pp. 78–9).

To the above list, it will be observed, Russia so far has con-
tributed only two examples.   It is highly probable that inquiry
in the proper quarters would reveal others in that country.
In spite of considerable search I have found no mention of any
such relic in Germany, and England too seems to have been
without one.[3]

By the Capuchins of Enghien the legend POΔION is
explained as [H]POΔION, ' coin of Herod '.   This fact seems
to favour M. de Mély's suggestion that in the superficial resemblance between the names of Herod and Rhodes lay the reason
for the association of these coins with the Thirty Pieces of Silver.
Otherwise why should so large a proportion of the relics (eight
out of the ten or eleven which can be identified) be of this particular

---

[1] *Italia Sacra* (1719), tome iv, cols. 27, 28.

[2] See *Delle antichità longobardico-milanesi illustr. con dissert. dai monaci della congreg. cisterciese di Lombardia*, iv (1793), pp. 285, 286 ; and H. J. Floss, *Dreikönigenbuch* (1864), p. 56.

[3] The late Sir W. H. St. John Hope confirmed me in this particular.

class ? M. Babelon, however, throws doubt on this hypothesis. He points out that Rouille makes no allusion to Herod, and has allowed his engraver to give the inscription as POAION (for POMAION) ; the text of the gospel gives no ground for thinking of coins of Herod. Further, he cites Mommsen as proving from an inscription that the coins of Rhodes even in Roman times were prized for their beauty. It must, however, be admitted that Mommsen's interpretation of the inscription goes beyond the evidence ; the Rhodian coins may have had a higher exchange value than others of the same weight, but we do not know that their beauty was the cause. In matters of this sort beauty counts for little. Probably the Rhodian coins had a reputation for purity. Again, the A in Rouille's engraving is doubtless a mere slip on the engraver's part ; he would not be the only engraver who, from ignorance of Greek, has made this mistake, nor Rouille the only numismatist who has allowed it to pass. Is not the word given as POΛION in one of the illustrations reproduced by M. de Mély from the work of Budaeus ? Again, the quantity of the *o* in Herod's name would, in those days, offer no obstacle to the identification. Nor has the objection drawn from the text of the gospel much force ; after all, ' pieces of silver ' could be interpreted as coins of Herod no less than as Roman coins. M. Babelon's first objection has more validity than the others. There is no trace of this connexion with Herod in any of the older literature. On some of the relics, as on that at Rhodes itself, we know that the inscription was quite obliterated. These then could not have been chosen because of the reason suggested by M. de Mély.

The true reason, after all, is a very simple one, and has only escaped notice because the presence of the specimen in the castle at Rhodes was not recorded by M. de Mély, on whose researches all subsequent discussion of the question has been based. It must be remembered that a very large number of the pilgrims to the Holy Land would see the relics in the Castle. Now Rhodian coins must have been as common in the Levant then as now, and, being of striking beauty, once seen were not easily forgotten. The pilgrim would thus recognize another Rhodian coin, if shown him, as similar to the one at Rhodes. Here then, to his mind, was a possible ' Judas-penny '. It was thus inevitable that many such pieces should find their way into shrines.

This theory seems to me to explain why so many Rhodian

coins figure in our list.   But, it will be asked, Why was the particular relic at Rhodes selected for the purpose ?   To this it might be answered, Why was the Egyptian dirhem or the Syracusan decadrachm chosen ?   But it is not necessary thus to evade the question.   As we have seen, the Rhodian church possessed at the end of the fourteenth century a gold coin of the Empress Helena, impressions or facsimiles of which, made under certain circumstances of peculiar solemnity, were of great virtue.   Now the Voyage du Seigneur d'Anglure, which mentions this gold coin of St. Helena in 1395, does not mention the silver 'Judas-penny'.   Conversely, the later authorities, beginning in 1413, who mention the 'Judas-penny', do not mention the coin of St. Helena.   Finally we learn that impressions were made of the 'Judas-penny' under the same circumstances and with the same effect as in the case of the coin of St. Helena.

The ' Judas-penny ' then, early in the fifteenth century, had taken the place of the gold coin of St. Helena.   And I think, on the evidence before us, we shall not be unjust to the knights in suggesting that, the latter having disappeared, the authorities found it necessary to have some other relic of equally miraculous properties.   They might perhaps have obtained one of the aurei of St. Helen which, as we have seen (p. 107, note), were found in Rome in 1398.   But if they were for any reason hard pressed, nothing could be easier to obtain in Rhodes than an ancient Rhodian coin ; and if the inscription on it were obliterated, so much the better.

In the light of the fact that reproductions in silver were made by people like Johann Tucher, particular interest attaches to a piece cast in silver and now preserved at Paris in the Cabinet des Médailles in the Bibliothèque Nationale.[1]   As will be seen from the illustration (fig. 65), we have a considerably debased [2] reproduction of a Rhodian coin of the kind with which we are familiar.   In the mould of the obverse have been added the words IMAGO CESARIS in lettering of the fifteenth century.   The man who added them obviously argued as follows : This coin, one of the thirty pence for which Christ was sold, must have been one

[1] Published by M. de Mély in Rev. Numism., 1901, pp. 262 ff.   M. de la Tour informed me that the piece is undoubtedly cast, not struck.   From Mr. L. O. Tudeer I learn that there is another specimen, also cast, in the University Collection at Helsingfors.

[2] So much debased in style that many reproductions must have intervened, one would think, between the original and this.

of those about which He asked the question, ' Whose image and superscription is this ? ' Therefore the head is that of Caesar, and the fact may as well be made clear in the reproductions which I am issuing.

In a painting of doubtful date, in the manner of Lucas van Leyden, referred to above (p. 87), the Thirty Pieces are represented by the imitations of the Jewish shekel which became popular early in the sixteenth century. It is curious that the genuine Jewish shekel and this much commoner imitation appear so rarely among the actual relics which have been identified.

Fig. 65.—Silver reproduction of fourth-century coin of Rhodes, fifteenth century.

Before the sixteenth century the Jewish shekel was probably quite unknown in Europe ; and doubtless most of the relics which we have discussed were acquired much earlier. Nevertheless it seems puzzling that no shrine availed itself in the sixteenth century of these imitations, which were undoubtedly regarded as genuine by the vast majority of people, then as now.

Having dealt with matters of fiction, it would be unreasonable did we not attempt to satisfy ourselves on the much more prosaic question : What were the coins actually in circulation in Judaea in the time of Christ ? Our choice lies practically between two kinds of silver coin.[1]

The piece which both English versions of the New Testa-

[1] M. de Villenoisy, by a curious reversion to the argument of Godfrey of Viterbo, suggests that the coins described by St. Matthew as τὰ τριάκοντα ἀργύρια (triginta argenteos) were really gold pieces, on the ground that argentum, argenteus had become synonymous with ' money ', without regard to the metal. This may be true of the collective noun τὸ ἀργύριον, but I do not think it can be proved of τὰ ἀργύρια in the sense of separate pieces of money. The author of the Narratio of Joseph of Arimathaea was, however, of M. de Villenoisy's opinion ; for, as Mr. Herbert informs me, according to this work (edited by Tischendorf, Evang. Apocr., 1853, p. 440, from a twelfth-century and other manuscripts) the Jews bribed Judas with τριάκοντα ἀργύρια χρυσίου. Of course no argument can be based on evidence of this date. Feis discusses the question of the thirty ἀργύρια at great length, and comes, on grounds which appear to me to be inadequate, to the conclusion that they were Roman denarii.

ment call a ' penny ' was the ordinary Roman silver denarius, worth about 9½*d*. The specimen here illustrated (fig. 68) shows on the obverse the laureate ' image ' of the Emperor Tiberius with his ' superscription ' TI(BERIVS) CAESAR DIVI AVG(VSTI) F(ILIVS) AVGVSTVS ; on the reverse is the Empress Livia seated, and the inscription PONTIF(EX) MAXIM(VS), completing the titles of Tiberius.

But it is much more probable that we have to look for the Thirty Pieces of Silver in another kind of coin, corresponding in weight to the shekel. Such coins were not issued at this time by any

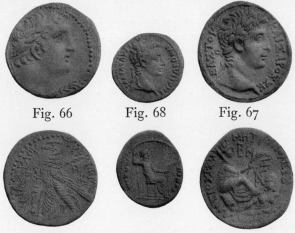

Fig. 66   Fig. 68   Fig. 67

Figs. 66–8.—Staters of Tyre and Antioch, and denarius of Tiberius
(British Museum).

mint in Judaea itself ; but the large silver four-drachm pieces of the mint of Tyre, weighing from 224 to 220 grains troy, and often less than this, were in common circulation. There were also coins, struck at the great city of Antioch on the Orontes, of which the weight sometimes rises as high as 236 grains troy. Such coins of Tyre or of Antioch are meant by the ' staters ' mentioned in the New Testament. Fig. 66, a four-drachm piece of Tyre, has on the obverse a laureate head of the Phoenician god Melkarth, who appears in his Hellenized form of Herakles. On the reverse is an eagle standing on the prow of a vessel, with a palm branch over its shoulder ; around is the name of the city, ' Tyre the sacred and inviolable sanctuary '. In front of the bird is a club, the emblem of the god whose head appears on the obverse. In the field of the coin are also a date (corresponding in this case to 4–3 B.C.) and a monogram differentiating this issue from others.

The staters of Antioch are better works of art than those of Tyre. On the obverse of the specimen in fig. 67 is a fine laureate head of Augustus, with the Greek inscription 'of Caesar Augustus'. On the reverse is represented the famous personification of the City of Antioch by the sculptor Eutychides : a female figure, wearing a mural crown, and holding a palm branch, seated on a rock ; at her feet is a half-figure of the river-god Orontes in a swimming attitude. The inscription around identifies the piece as a coin 'of the metropolis of the Antiochians ', and letters in the field fix its date to A.D. 11.

To one of these two classes, Tyrian or Antiochian, then, belonged not only the stater which was taken out of the mouth of the fish, and which, being equivalent in weight to a shekel, was sufficient to pay the tax for two people ; but also probably the thirty pieces of silver, which altogether must have been equivalent to something between £4 10s. and £5 in our money.

ADDENDA

Mr. H. H. E. Craster kindly calls my attention to two short poems by the fourteenth-century writer Nicephorus Callistus (see above, p. 10) contained in a Bodleian manuscript (MS. Auct. E. 5. 14 = cod. misc. 79 in Coxe's Catalogue) contemporary with the author. The poems (which are mentioned by Krumbacher, *Byz. Litteraturgesch.*, 2e. Aufl., p. 292) celebrate two gems bearing portraits of Christ : a crystal, and an amethyst made to the order of the Emperor. It is not clear whether they were intaglios or cameos. With Olga's stone (p. 33) we thus know of three Byzantine gems with the portrait of Christ in addition to the emerald sent to the Vatican.

Mr. J. Leveen makes a new suggestion concerning the *crux* of the Hebrew inscription (p. 53). As it reaches me too late for insertion in the proper place, I am glad to be able to record it here. ' A reading of these letters which has not been suggested is ואך מאדם. If we examine the final kaph of מלך we see that the letter which is assumed to be a ד or ר can also be read as a final kaph. There are two translations possible of this new reading : (1) " and only from a man " ; (2) " and only from blood ". The word for " blood " in New Hebrew is אדם or אדמא as well as the biblical דם.'

INDEX

I. GENERAL

II. INSCRIPTIONS

PRINTED IN ENGLAND
AT THE OXFORD UNIVERSITY PRESS